RAISING OLIVES IN PROVENCE

Also by Kenneth R. Timmerman

Nonfiction

*And the Rest Is History: Tales of Hostages, Arms Dealers,
Dirty Tricks, and Spies*

*Deception: The Making of the YouTube Video Hillary
and Obama Blamed for Benghazi*

Dark Forces: The Truth about What Happened in Benghazi

Shadow Warriors: Traitors, Saboteurs, and the Party of Surrender

Countdown to Crisis: The Coming Nuclear Showdown with Iran

The French Betrayal of America

Preachers of Hate: Islam and the War on America

Shakedown: Exposing the Real Jesse Jackson

Selling Out America: The American Spectator Investigations

The Death Lobby: How the West Armed Iraq

Fiction

The Election Heist

Isis Begins

Honor Killing

The Wren Hunt

www.kentimmerman.com

RAISING OLIVES IN PROVENCE

A Guide for Body and Soul

Kenneth R. Timmerman

Post Hill
PRESS

A POST HILL PRESS BOOK

Raising Olives in Provence:
A Guide for Body and Soul
© 2023 by Kenneth R. Timmerman
All Rights Reserved

ISBN: 979-8-88845-160-1
ISBN (eBook): 979-8-88845-161-8

Cover concept by Stephen Hall
Cover image by Pierre-August Renoir, *La danse à Bougival (1883)*
Interior design and composition by Greg Johnson, Textbook Perfect

Post Hill Press
New York • Nashville
posthillpress.com

Published in the United States of America
1 2 3 4 5 6 7 8 9 10

For Albert Velli,
faithful friend and companion
1938–2009

Life is good
God is great
And Jesus is not a Muslim.

Contents

We Get Hooked 1

Girls and Horses. 5

Ofilio and the Cistern. 7

Just Earn More Money, Husband!. 16

Angélus 19

At Least You Can Give Me Some More Wine 21

Will She Love Him When He's Poor? 23

Sleeping with the Boar. 29

Cat Invasion 32

Bay of Pigs 38

Les Mandarines 43

Asterix and Obelix. 45

I Will Cut It Off 51

What Real Men Do on Their Vacation 57

Fire! 65

Boar Hunt 73

The Artist 79

The End of Something 82

The Truffle Market. 86

We Are Rich. 91

Land of the Lotus Eaters. 95

Finding the Pony 100

First Harvest 105

Le Jour du Merci Donnant 113

Pruning 119

Le Pipe. 122

The Sailing Club 126

Le Club 55. 131

A Jew from Alexandria 138

Deliverance. 144

Bouillie Bordelaise 153

Alexis Meets His Match. 157

The Regatta. 160

The Olive Thief 166

Albert 178

Seasonal Pleasures. 184

Plucked Like a Pigeon 195

Fish Day. 201

More Trees 205

The Man Who Beat Trump 210

Little Cookie 220

The Cast-Iron Lunch 238

L'Envoi 244

About the Author 248

We Get Hooked

We never dreamed of finding olive trees on the property when we first walked through the crumbling stone archway on top of the hillside and discovered the view that literally took our breaths away. It wasn't just the deep blue of the Mediterranean in the distance, wedged between two hills. Nor was it the vastness of the sky, the majestic cork oaks, or the valley below the house with its vineyards, olive orchards, and cypress sentinels that could have been painted by Cézanne. It was the whole setting: the bumpy dirt track leading up the isolated hillside that rocked us against the doors of the real estate agent's car, the wildness and utter emptiness of the *maquis*, the

foreboding mountains just beyond, and then suddenly discovering the crumbling stone archway with its old tarnished bell bearing the promise that some island of civilization lay just beyond.

We had been staying that autumn at a Swedish friend's house in Beauvallon, about fifteen minutes from Saint-Tropez, so I could finish a book. Our two youngest children were attending the local French schools. When we decided to

1

prolong our stay in Europe that summer, Christina reasoned that we would never have a better opportunity for them to learn French properly. Another year and Diana would be entering high school, making it far more complicated to change school systems, let alone languages. Simon, four years her junior, was still of an age where school was more day care than education, and at any rate, he had inherited an adventurous streak and an ability to make friends anywhere in any language (as we had seen a few summers earlier when vacationing in the Cyclades in Greece). There was no pressing reason for us to return to the Washington, DC, suburbs. I had a good contract for the book, a decent laptop, and could write anywhere. *Why not just stay in Europe?* Christina reasoned. After all, four of our five children had been born in either Sweden or France. In many ways, it already was our second home.

As Christmas and the end of our six months in Beauvallon approached, all four of us were overcome by a sense of the specialness of our circumstances. Reality—in the form of American public schools, endless driving on the Washington, DC, Beltway, and the demands of work—was about to come crashing down on our heads. If our long walks up and down the hillsides and through the vineyards with Churchill, our yellow Lab, had been our way of getting acquainted with our temporary surroundings in Beauvallon, house-hunting became our psychological prop, our gimmick to keep reality at bay.

We never thought we would buy a house in Provence. Not seriously. We had some money saved, but we had never had a discussion of how we would finance a second home. It was just a dream, a pastime, a way of learning more about a region of France that both of us loved—until we walked through that crumbling stone archway.

"It's a bit far from the village," the real estate agent was saying. "And it's a bit more expensive than the other places I have shown you. But I thought at least you should see it. It has just come on the market this week because of an inheritance."

Christina said nothing. After all, she is a Swede and has that flinty quality born of harsh winters and short, glorious summers that give

Swedes the ability to appear detached, even bored, at moments of high emotion. But I could tell from the flare of her nostrils, the slight opening of her lips, and the sudden intake of breath that she was thrilled.

She was also at heart a businesswoman and didn't want to let on to the real estate agent that we might actually be interested in this ridiculously expensive cold stone house on an isolated hillside with its overgrown yard and tiny pool. And so far from the sea!

"This is our dream house," she whispered to me in Swedish.

"The beach must be a good ten kilometers away," I said.

"Yes, that's true," the agent said. "But you told me you weren't interested in any of those pink villas by the sea."

I was almost grinding my teeth. The real estate agent, whose name was Véronique Bardot, told us that she was related through her ex-husband to the famous French film star Brigitte Bardot, who had contributed to making Saint-Tropez the haven of the rich and famous. Judging from our cool response to that information, she immediately deduced that the Tropezian lifestyle was not something we envied. In other words, this place was perfect for us. She had us on the hook, and she knew it.

"There's no way we could afford it," I said, looking at the spec sheet for the property.

"Maybe not. But it's always fun to look. *Qu'en pensez-vous,* madame? What do you think?"

Christina gave me an abandoned look and laughed.

"It's spectacular. If we were ever going to buy something here, this would be it," she said. "We'll never find anything like it again."

Later, back at our Swedish friend's pink villa by the sea, we attempted to have a rational discussion.

"It's more than twice the price of the other places she showed us," I ventured.

"But they were horrible."

"It has no kitchen. I mean, it's the 1950s!"

"You can build the kitchen."

3

"Seriously. There's nothing. No cabinets, no countertops. And those horrible tiles on the floor."

But she wasn't hearing any of it. "You like to do tile," she said. "Besides, it will give you something to take your mind off your writing."

Girls and Horses

Our children were having the time of their lives, and that certainly added to the underlying desire we dared not admit to buy a house of our own in Provence. Simon and Diana were sailing at Sainte-Maxime with their schools, which still retained the old French tradition of Wednesday afternoons off so the children could go to catechism classes (even though in post-Christian Europe, catechism was a thing of the past). Simon was tiny then. I think he knew that Christina had decided he would be her last, and so he stayed small for as long as he could. But he was strong and proudly carried the sail for his Optimist over his head to the beach, where an instructor would attach it to the hull of the small boat. The Gulf of Saint-Tropez was the ideal place to learn to sail. The winds were perfect and always brought the tiny one-person boats back to shore when the afternoon lesson was over, bobbing behind the instructor's Zodiac like a row of baby ducks. Their summer tans deepened through the autumn, and by Thanksgiving, they were bronzed like gods.

On the weekends when we weren't visiting friends or off on some excursion, such as a bullfight in Arles or canoeing through the Gorges du Verdon, Diana would ride horses in the plain of Grimaud with her mother.

Christina was a horsewoman. She had been raised on a farm south of Stockholm and had been a miserable student at Diana's age, preferring to romp in the woods with ponies and boys instead of studying. Her mother finally understood the trick and offered to buy her a thoroughbred if she did better in the eighth grade. Almost overnight she went from being a below-average student who struggled in class to getting almost straight As. Later, her passion for horses nearly convinced her to abandon political science and a promising government career in Stockholm to become a veterinarian. Divorce from her first husband and the need to earn a living cured her of that.

"Anders used to complain that I was married to my horse," she said.

"I can sympathize with that."

"But there was never any competition."

"Try to convince a man of that," I said.

Until recently, she had pretty much given up riding, except for summers in Sweden when she visited her thoroughbred mare, Dolette, which she had given to her best friend from university. When we first lived in France, we didn't have the money for her to ride; once we moved to America nine years ago and were raising five children, she had no time.

But this autumn she started to ride again in Grimaud, accompanying Diana on her middle school equestrian outings. She didn't talk about it much—only about Diana and her crazy French instructor, who was named Tristan.

"He had them jump over obstacles that were higher than a fence," she said. "Nobody would even think of having you do such a thing in Sweden. And here is this French guy, standing there shouting at these twelve-year-old girls with hardly any training: *Allez! Allez! Allez!* And so they just went and jumped. And nobody thought anything about it."

It was outrageous, and it was wonderful. She made it almost sound like a great crime, but that was her way. No one got hurt, so we all laughed. Diana was always flushed with excitement when she came home from the riding lessons, and I was too dumb to understand that in telling the story of her daughter's adventures, Christina was really conveying her longing to ride again.

Ofilio and the Cistern

We went back several times in the weeks before Christmas, and there was no hope: we were smitten. The more we learned about the property and the Swedish match magnate who had designed and built it in the early 1960s, the more the boom of fate seemed to swing in our direction, forcing us to duck and shift our weight to accommodate its new tack or get swept away into the sea of lost hopes and unrealized dreams.

Madame Bardot was careful to warn us about the water.

"You will probably have to drill a new well," she said. "The one that's here is insufficient, and the natural springs have gone dry."

Helping her to explain the property was a local stonemason named Ofilio Castellane. Ofilio was the caretaker for the three heirs to the property. He had keys to the gate in the archway. Keys to the tower. Keys to the main house, the pool room, the garage, the cellars, the metal security shutters. Everything was locked, and each key had its own tag, written in Ofilio's rough block letters. He kept them in a sturdy plastic bag. He was Master of the Keys.

Ofilio had worked for the deceased owner, a French widow who lived in New Caledonia but spent the summers here after her husband died. For years, Ofilio had been responsible for clearing the thick brush around the house to protect it from the forest fires that periodically ravaged the region and for handling whatever maintenance needed to be done. Short, solidly built, with the rough hands of one who does manual work, Ofilio was also an entrepreneur. He told us that he managed several properties down in the village and would be happy to add ours to his rental offerings—for a fee, of course. Although it was clear he was angling for our business, we began doing mental calculations and realized that by renting out the house six to eight weeks per year we could cover a significant portion of our mortgage payments. All of a sudden a wild dream began to appear within reach.

"What's the problem with the well?" I asked him as we were doing a walk round the house to look at the septic system. I was learning things about leach fields and dry-well ventilation I had never expected to care about.

"There's not enough water," Ofilio said dismissively.

"Why is that?"

"There's not enough water!" he repeated, thickening his Provençal accent to indicate what an idiot these foreigners were not to understand something that should be self-evident.

"Why is there not enough water?" I persisted. "Did they drill the well in the wrong place? Are there too many other wells in the same aquifer? Is the climate changing?"

Ofilio just threw up his hands, completely fed up with my refusal to take his proclamation as writ. "I'm telling you, you're going to need a second well. I can get you an estimate, if you like."

So that was it. Ofilio had a buddy who was in the well-drilling business, and he wanted us as clients. He would be caretaker of the property and clear the brush and handle the renters. All these services had a fee. He saw us as pigeons that had flown unwittingly into his coop. He was planning to pluck us slowly and often.

Madame Bardot became my secret ally in dealing with Ofilio. It turned out that she hadn't been able to get any answers out of him either, but because she was local, she couldn't press him as I could.

At my insistence, he took us to examine the pump house at the bottom of the driveway, just inside the gates. The metal door was stiff on the hinges, and Ofilio needed to kick away dirt and stones to get it to open. It was a tiny structure, so low you had to crouch to get inside, which I did. There was an electrical control box and a single pipe at the far end that looped from the ground to a hole in the wall leading toward the hill.

"How does the water get from the well to the house?" I asked. He was standing outside the door and bent toward me slightly.

"Cistern," he said.

"How big is it?"

"Thirty thousand liters. When it gets below a certain point, it triggers the pump. It works automatically."

I had no clue how a cistern could trigger a pump in a distant well; all I knew about cisterns was what I had seen in Roman ruins in Europe and Jerusalem. I figured that if we were actually going to buy this property, I'd better learn as much as I could about it.

"Where is the cistern?" I asked him as I crawled out of the pump house.

"Up there." He waved vaguely. Glum. He was beginning to catch my drift.

"Where up there?" I asked.

"It's far."

"It's on the property, right?"

Véronique stepped in. "Oh, yes. Monsieur Castellane knows exactly where it is. He's been maintaining the property for many years. He's the one who knows all those details. If you have questions, you need to ask him."

She gave me a mischievous smile, as we both could hear Ofilio cursing under his breath.

"Let's go have a look," I said.

"It hasn't been cleared," Ofilio said. "We'd have to walk."

To Ofilio, that was a showstopper. Even though it was early December, it was still around seventy degrees Fahrenheit, and the sun burned through our clothes. Clearly to Ofilio, crashing through the brush in the midday heat was something that nobody in their right mind would do. But to me, it was an invitation. I love to walk, and the heat has never deterred me. After twenty-five years of carrying children on my back along rocky paths in Greece at the height of summer, the idea of venturing up to discover my own cistern on my own hillside sounded like a pleasant romp before lunch.

"If you really want to go up there, just follow the old road. It starts beyond the gate to the left."

I was gazing in awe at the dense underbrush that rose steeply above the driveway, wondering just how much of it was part of the property. There was a total of around sixteen acres, cut like a jigsaw puzzle through other landholdings. Véronique had shown me a map, but there were no landmarks I could recognize, and I had no way of gauging distances. From down here, the maquis appeared like a thick carpet of greenery, broken by the carbuncled black spines and lollipop tops of the cork oaks. Up above there was a stand of sea pines and an occasional mimosa. Somewhere in the midst of that was the cistern.

"How long does it take to get up there?" I asked.

"*Bof!*" he said. It was a gesture of exasperation, dismissive and a bit contemptuous.

"How long?" I pressed.

"Perhaps ten or fifteen minutes. You might want to wear gloves."

"I have some in my car," Véronique offered.

"We need you to show us the way," I said to Ofilio.

Now he was absolutely beside himself. "*Putaign!*" he said in his thick Provençal accent, not so quietly. I don't think he cared whether I understood the curse or not.

"They are serious buyers, Monsieur Castellane," said Véronique. "They certainly have a right to know what is on the property." She and Christina exchanged a knowing smile like two cats sharing a canary.

With Ofilio grudgingly leading the way, we headed down to the bottom of the driveway and waited while he scoured the maquis along the dirt access road, looking for the path. After a bit, he stopped and pointed into the dense thicket. When we joined him, he gave us the verdict.

"It hasn't been cleared in several years. Are you sure you want to go up there?"

"Absolutely," I said.

So, with Ofilio slowly pushing through the tall brush, we started up the steep incline. Most of the maquis was heather, with dense wooly foliage and trunks as thick as a man's ankle, and white or pink cistus, an oily plant similar to the turpentine bush that grows in the American South. But we also pressed through thickets of mature Scotch broom, careful to avoid the heavy thorns. Ofilio had pulled a pair of gloves out of his hip pocket and let the branches fall back behind him without a glance to us, punctuating his progress with a stream of obscenities, his bitter monologue of contempt.

After about a hundred meters, Ofilio cut back in the other direction, and all of a sudden, most of the brush disappeared and we could see the white and ochre rocks of what appeared to be a road.

"He must have let it grow down below so no one would come up here," Véronique whispered. She was puffing and sweating, but not unhappy to have bested Ofilio in our little standoff. She was learning his ways just as we were.

The road made another switchback, then traversed the hillside at an angle. There were so many rocks that the brush struggled to grow on most of the road itself. It looked like we were climbing a cantilevered dry streambed, although—if we were to believe Ofilio—there was no water up here.

Finally we reached a small clearing off to the side and Ofilio stopped.

"So where's the cistern?" I asked.

"You're standing on it."

So this was it? There was nothing to see. I started to walk around the clearing and almost fell off the side into the thicket.

"That's the edge," he said after I grabbed onto a tree branch. He was smirking as he pointed. "It goes from there, to there, and back around."

Several mimosa trees were beginning to bloom, crowding the view with thick bunches of small yellow fuzz balls. Véronique parted them and pointed out the house down below.

"It *is* far!" she said. "It must be over twelve hundred meters from here. So the water gets pumped up to here from the well, then goes down through the forest from here to the house."

"Carried by gravity," I said. "It's brilliant."

"You can tell he was a Swede," said Christina.

"A brilliant Swede," I added.

She was referring to the mysterious Stenberg, who had built the house and designed the water system. Ofilio was crouching down, fiddling with his bag of keys, trying to find the one that opened a heavy padlock seemingly embedded in the dirt. When he did, he stood up again and cleared dirt away with his boot, revealing a square metal panel attached at the back to a set of rusty hinges.

"Are you sure you want me to open it?" he said.

"Of course!"

I was excited, and so were Christina and Véronique. None of us had a clue what we would find when Ofilio lifted the access door. Was it a gateway with steps leading down to an underground chamber? Or a bottomless pit teaming with spiders, scorpions, and snakes? He needed both hands to lift the panel, not because it was so large or heavy but because the hinges had rusted shut and the cement holding them started to move, threatening to break. So he eased the panel back and forth until it creaked upward, so rusty that it stayed up by itself. I bent forward to look inside and recoiled from the stench.

"What's that?" I asked Ofilio.

He shrugged. "It's a cistern. The house has been empty for over a year, so there's no point."

"No point in what?"

"You've got to throw chlorine in regularly to kill the bacteria from the mice."

Once my eyes adjusted, I followed a ray of sunshine to the bottom of the cistern, around eight feet below us. The water came only about halfway up. Causing the stench that rose from below was a large mess of rotting fur and flesh on top of the water. You could still see the tail and the toes of the dead mouse.

"Do you get mice in your cisterns on the farm in Sweden?" I asked Christina.

"Rarely," she said. "We have proper lids to keep them out."

"I guess this is what they did in the Old Testament when they talked about poisoning the wells. The original biological warfare."

Ofilio was sweating, but finally he seemed actually happy. We had seen for ourselves that he had been right all along. Surely we must now see that our curiosity had been stupid and naïve.

"That's why you need another well," he said. "Like I said, there's not enough water."

"But wait," I said. "Didn't you say there was a natural spring?"

"Two of them, actually—according to the property registry," Véronique added.

She was throwing down the gauntlet, and I wondered how Ofilio was going to respond. Another temper tantrum about the heat and the maquis and how hard it was to get up the hill?

"They have been dry for years. Nobody even knows anymore where they are."

"You're saying *you* don't know where they are?"

As I blurted this out, I could see that I was getting close to the red line. If he was going to maintain his status as Master of the Keys, he needed to demonstrate that he alone knew the secrets of the property.

"Of course I know. They're up in the ravine. But no one has cleared a path up there since the last fire, and that was ten years ago. What's left of the basins will be clogged with vines. It's a lot of work, and no one's sure if there's water anymore. It's easier to dig another well."

Far from being turned off by finding the rotting mouse in the cistern, I was fascinated by the idea that somewhere buried in the wilderness of the hillside were two natural springs, sources of deep underground water. In French, the word for natural spring is *source*. As a writer and an investigative reporter, it was a word that resonated with me far beyond the literal meaning. It evoked deep underground caverns where all creation began, dripping off damp walls to form hidden pools, the murmuring of untold spirits. I could feel the beginnings of a proprietary instinct, that ancient attachment to land. Water was so precious here in this sun-parched wilderness that having control over two natural springs was a godsend. I, who had never particularly enjoyed drinking water, was about to taste the delicacies of these natural *sources*, to dip my toes in the living water of life. Did he say *challenge*?

As we walked back down, Ofilio way out in front so we couldn't pester him with more questions, Véronique stopped and pointed up the hillside and laughed. "It's like *Manon des Sources*," she said, referring to the famous novel by Marcel Pagnol about Provence in the early twentieth century. It was a tale of scarce water, gothic intrigue, and revenge and was familiar to all who lived here. (Indeed, how many young couples named their first girl-child Manon?) "You've got it all. The local characters who resent the foreigner moving in, the unexpected riches he finds beneath the ground. Really, I hope you are able to pull together the finances. If I had the money, I would almost buy this place myself!"

Just Earn More Money, Husband!

Since early childhood, I have had premonitions of things to come. In college, I studied Jung, Freud, and Groddeck and came to believe that in dreams, one could visit the actual future or far distant past, as if there were a parallel universe or state of being where they were all present at once, like a ladder going up and down through time.

My mentor in graduate school, the novelist John Hawkes, liked to say "fiction precedes reality." I never understood that as anything more than a cute elitist trope until I wrote the climactic scene in my first published novel, *The Wren Hunt*. In the book, the main character dons an old-fashioned diving suit and descends into the sunken streets of a "rose city" off the coast of an imaginary Mediterranean island. While he is underwater, his rival tries to murder him by severing the air hose. He survives—but just barely—in what I intended to be a variation of the pagan death/rebirth rituals I was studying at the time. Everyone who read the book loved that scene and asked me where they could find the rose city. But of course, I didn't have a clue. I had made it all up.

A few years later, during one of our summer trips to Greece, Christina and I visited the island of Kimolos, home to sea captains, stray cats, and a few goat farmers and winegrowers. There were no cars except in the main town, and the best beaches were on the far side of the island, an hour-and-a-half walk along a rocky path through rolling vineyards and fig trees and stone ruins. But once we reached that beach, the magic began. Snorkeling out some fifty meters from the sandy shore, I discovered beneath the shallow waters what seemed to be a clear pattern in the yellowish rose-colored stone. Could it be city streets and ruined houses, covered with generations of mollusks and sludge? It was all too regular to be random. Later, questioning the locals in the village, we learned that an ancient city built on a promontory over the beach had slid into the sea when the volcano on Thera (Santorini) exploded around 1500 BC. That was when I understood what John Hawkes meant when he said fiction precedes reality. The rose city was real, not just a projection of my imagination.

Over the years, the premonitions and artistic vision I believed in as a younger man have given way to more traditional Christian beliefs, not out of doctrine but out of experience. I believe that God has a plan for each and every one of us. Although there are billions of us on Earth, it is a personal plan and has been tailored for our individual circumstances and our life's journey. That's how great he is, how vast and incomprehensible. In any single instant of human time, he can grasp the individual destinies of billions of people all at once without breaking a sweat. And he is a stickler for details! If we came upon this place on a hillside in the south of France, it was part of God's plan for the two of us. He puts obstacles in our way to test us and mature us. He is there in our suffering. And yes, he also grants rewards. But like the suffering, God's bounty is just a means for us to better accomplish his purpose. It is up to us to seek his purpose and to use his bounty toward his greater glory.

As Christina and I began to go through our finances, we realized that we had tucked away money in lots of different places over the years and had more savings than we thought. Added to this was the state of the euro, which was still struggling four years after its introduction in January 1999 and had just regained parity with the dollar after a deep slide. When we put everything on the table, we had nearly 50 percent of the purchase price of the house, more than enough to meet the French down payment requirement of 20 percent...if—a big if—we could finance the rest. The French were far more conservative lenders than the US banks, as we knew from financing our previous house in the Paris suburb of Maisons-Laffitte.

"You should be fine," Véronique told us. "I will introduce you to a banker I work with. Let's see what he can come up with."

Was it possible that God really wanted us to fulfill our dream of coming back to France—not permanently, but as temporary residents, with the luxury of owning a second home? For someone who has struggled financially all his life, I could hardly believe it. And yet, every time we bumped up against what I thought should have been a closed door, it stood wide open. It was as if this *was* his plan and that he wanted to shower us with gifts. I was beginning to feel we were being drawn forward by strong, sure hands, guiding and protecting us.

"How are we ever going to pay for this?" Christina wondered when the banker had left the pink villa we were renting after several hours of filling out loan documents.

"If this is God's will, he will provide. Look how he watches over the sparrows in the air or the lilies in the field. Surely if he can care about them, he cares about you, about us.

"Just earn more money, husband."

We drank some more of the rough, simple wine from the vineyard in nearby Grimaud and began to picture ourselves in this new place. I loved Christina's rough, simple outlook on life. She always forced me to get real.

Angélus

Christina's ex-sister-in-law came to visit us a few days after Christmas while we were still in Beauvallon. Mona was in her mid-sixties and had spent thirty-five years married to the wrong man. With our moral support, she finally divorced him two years earlier and was hoping to revive her creative talents, which she had put on ice throughout her long and often violent marriage. As a young woman, the daughter of a famous Swedish diplomat, she had a promising career as a celebrity photographer. But once she married Guy, a star architect whose career was riding a rocket of fame, she set her own ambitions aside. For years, he brutalized her emotionally and physically, chasing other women while expecting her to stay home with their children. He would disappear for days on an orgy of alcohol and sex, spending huge sums on nightclubs, limousines, and gifts for his latest flame. Then he would return home, hungover and broke, and berate her because they were poor. It happened again and again, year after year, with Levitical predictability. I don't know how many times Mona crashed at our place in despair, wanting to leave Guy yet afraid she would destroy him if she did. "He's really just a child pretending to be grown up," she said once. We finally convinced her to stop making excuses, find a lawyer, and sue for divorce.

Mona was one of the most thoroughly good people I have ever met. With Guy, she was always blaming herself and wondering what she could do to rescue their marriage. She had a soul like mist that lingers over the earth after a rain, only to be burned away by the sun. It's a wonder Mona survived the real world. She was devoted to her children, now in their twenties, and lived in a tiny Paris studio on money she inherited from her mother and whatever Guy decided to give her in cash. Now she had started to write illustrated children's books.

She brought us her firstborn, called *Angélus*. It was beautiful, simple, and profound. It told the story of an angel who adopted a pet human. The human was always doing self-destructive things, but Angélus managed to arrive just in time to prevent the worst from happening. At one point, the angels compared notes on their pet humans and commiserated with Angélus. What a lousy human he got stuck with!

Much later, I learned Mona's story. She and Guy had a second son who died when he was three. "I can still see him, standing in his crib with this angelic smile," Christina said. "He had a childhood cancer. When he learned to talk, he used to say that he couldn't go out and run around like other children because he was going to die soon. Mona and Guy never got over his death."

We took Mona to visit the house one glorious afternoon in late December when the sun made the cork oaks shimmer. In the distance, we could see the lighthouse above Sainte-Maxime and the ocean beyond, a pool of deep blue held in place by the sloping hills. Mona caught her breath in that typically Swedish way, half astonishment, half punctuation, sexy and pure all at once.

"This is your paradise, Ken," she said. "You must come to write your books here. This is meant to be."

All of a sudden it clicked. Our natural springs, a gift of God in this parched land where water is so precious, and Mona's imaginary guardian angel. We decided to call the house Les Sources d'Angélus.

Angelus Springs.

At Least You Can Give Me
Some More Wine

The early months of 2003 were momentous, if one happened to be following the news. The drumbeats of war that had been steadily building reached fever pitch as the world prepared to punish Saddam Hussein. But this was very different from the first Gulf War. For one, Saddam hadn't done something so obvious as invade another country. That made determining how severe a threat he posed a question of intelligence, interpretation, and judgment.

On a personal level, I had friends who were now senior officials in the administration and others who were leaders of the Iraqi opposition who were willing to share what was going on behind the scenes. Since I had just finished correcting the galleys of *Preachers of Hate*, my book on Islam and the terrorist war on America, I threw myself into reporting on the buildup to this new war with feverish intensity. One of the first pieces I wrote exposed a joint effort by the State Department and CIA to disembowel the Iraqi opposition. I found this curious, since my Pentagon sources were telling me that the war plan called for the US to oust Saddam, then stand up a new Iraqi government *run by* the opposition.[1]

---

[1] Kenneth R. Timmerman, "Does State Have a Post-Saddam Strategy?" *Insight*, Feb. 4, 2003. http://www.kentimmerman.com/news/iraq_inc_0203.htm.

Then came the French. Secretary of State Colin Powell thought he had worked out a deal with his "good friend" Dominique Galouzeau de Villepin, the French foreign minister, for France to join the coalition against Saddam. Instead, Villepin held a surprise press conference in New York, where he announced that France would never support a US-led military intervention against Saddam. When Powell saw him on the video monitors at the UN, his jaw dropped. He couldn't believe that Villepin could be so duplicitous.

Thus began the era of "freedom fries," Air Force One servings of "freedom toast," and bad French jokes. Former undersecretary of defense Jed Babbin put a wickedly simple spin on it: "Going to war without France is like going deer hunting without an accordion. You leave a lot of useless noisy baggage behind."[2]

One night at dinner at the end of January, I turned to Christina half in despair.

"If we hadn't made the ten percent down payment, I'd be ready to cancel the whole thing," I said. "Buy a house in France? Are we mad? I don't think things have ever been this bad."

"We still haven't been approved for the loan," she said.

That was true. Plus, we had asked to increase the amount because the euro had appreciated significantly over the past month.

"If they turn us down, that's it," I said.

Christina said nothing. After a moment, she jiggled her empty wine glass.

"If we're not going to have a house in France, at least you can give me some more wine."

---

[2] Babbin made that comment on January 30, 2003, on MSNBC's *Hardball with Chris Matthews*. The description of Powell's shock at Villepin's treachery comes from my 2004 book, *The French Betrayal of America* (Crown Forum). In that book (pages 189–192), I also describe the real reason the French didn't go along with the US-led war against Saddam: a $100 billion agreement to develop Iraq's oil fields that Saddam conditioned upon French help in getting UN sanctions on Iraq lifted.

Will She Love Him When He's Poor?

In the end, the French bank not only approved our loan but gave us a terrific rate. We were set to close on the house on March 17, 2003—just days before the war in Iraq began in earnest. I was reluctant to leave Washington, which, as always during a world crisis, had become the political omphalos. What once had seemed like it was destined by God now seemed like a really bad idea. I knew from living and working in France for eighteen years as a journalist that no "rule of law" could protect you if you aroused the ire of the French state for whatever reason, no matter how petty. If the French wanted to punish someone, they unleashed the state. There were enough unpopular taxes, obscure rules, and hidden regulations to make everyone a criminal. I was worried we were headed for disaster.[3]

I arrived on the morning of the seventeenth at Nice Côte d'Azur Airport and drove along the coast from Saint-Raphaël to Sainte-Maxime, where I had an appointment with Madame Bardot. The last stretch of road as you enter Sainte-Maxime is spectacular. It curves above the shoreline, twisting around hidden coves, with giant wind-battered umbrella pines growing at precarious angles right out of an Edvard Munch painting. High stone walls shroud lavish villas,

---

[3] The French attempted to expel me in 1992 on phony espionage charges because I'd inadvertently helped block a major arms deal. See *And the Rest Is History*, chapter 12, "Persona Non Grata."

and everything is splashed with mounds of white and pink oleander and crimson bougainvillea.

"What a strange situation," said Madame Bardot. We had grown to know each other well enough that we now exchanged three kisses on the cheek. "I hope you don't think people here hate America. Remember: Provence is not Paris."

"Thankfully," I said.

"No, really. You will see *chez le notaire*."

In France, all real estate deals get signed in the notary's office, and he takes a stiff commission for handling the paperwork and providing what amounts to a title search and title insurance.

"It's only politics," she went on. "It will pass. Everyone here thinks that Chirac and Villepin have lost their minds. Oppose the United States? Whatever for?"

I followed her in my rental car around the Gulf of Saint-Tropez, past the stately palm trees of Beauvallon where we had stayed in the autumn, around the traffic circle at the Géant Casino, past the polo field and the pottery lots and the cane brakes wracked by the winter winds, until we reached the outskirts of town. This time of year, there was hardly any traffic, but in the summer, the thirty-minute drive to Saint-Tropez can take two hours. The plane trees in town had been pruned, so their giant shorn trunks looked like closed fists and caught the spring sun like pieces of a shimmering mosaic. We parked at the port and walked together along the moorings to the notary's office. It was around sixteen degrees Celsius, dry and beautiful. Things were starting to look better, indeed.

"Have you ever noticed the name of the main road leading down to Pampelonne?" Véronique asked. Pampelonne was the most famous of the beaches of the peninsula (known as the Presqu'ile de Saint-Tropez) and stretched nearly two miles between headlands, forming a protected bay where the very wealthy would moor their yachts in summer so they could be seen by the envious having lunch at the overpriced beach clubs. "It's called the Boulevard Patch, and it's named after the American who liberated Provence, General Alexander Patch."

We knew vaguely about the August 15, 1944, landing in Provence—called Operation Dragoon because a reluctant Winston Churchill claimed he had to be "dragooned" into it—if only because we had discovered huge sheets of corrugated iron from a sunken landing craft one day while snorkeling after strong currents had brushed the sand away. It was one of the most overlooked operations of the entire war—not even the French made a big deal of it, I had always thought—since the main battle to liberate France from Nazi occupation was fought in the north, not here.

"You know the traffic circle before you come into Sainte-Maxime from Saint-Raphaël? The one that leads up to the golf club? That's called the Route du Débarquement," she went on. The word means "landing," as in Normandy and D-Day. "Almost every town between Cap Nègre and Saint-Raphaël has its monument to the Americans who landed here," she said. "We still commemorate the liberation every year. So you won't find people here to be anti-American. We owe our freedom to you."

Véronique was *such* a smart real estate agent. But in truth, she had no mercantile need to play to my patriotic sentiments at this point since the deal was done. I thought her comments were sincere.

The notary's *cabinet* was just beyond the plane trees at the head of town. It smelled of old France, old stone, and buried money. Maître Bortolotti liked old, dark furniture, and he was an older man whose skin had been darkened by scores of summers in the hot Provençal sun. This was the first time I met the sellers. The three brothers inherited the property from their mother, who in turn had bought it in the mid-1970s from Stenberg, the brilliant Swede. One of the brothers lived at the other end of the planet in New Caledonia, and another lived in New York, so the only one who came was Jean-Jacques. He lived in Paris and had just gotten engaged to the woman of his dreams, a buxomly blonde with a low-cut blouse, large sunglasses, and a floppy hat who made it clear she preferred cold, hard cash to a rustic property in the south of France that didn't even have a grassy lawn—*une pelouse*.

Maître Bortolotti presided over the ceremony like a justice of the peace over a wedding in the days when such ceremonies were not measured in half-minute increments. (In Sweden, we had the "long" ceremony in the chandeliered, oak-paneled reception hall in Stockholm's Stadshuset. It lasted all of three minutes.) He insisted on reciting the entire history of the property, and for such a recent acquisition, it had quite a pedigree. Stenberg was a serious investor and had studied the local families who owned the hillsides, buying up small parcels of land as someone died or someone else got married and lost interest in their inheritance. He took nearly ten years before he built the house in the early 1960s and kept buying small parcels for years afterward. As Bortolotti read out the lineage of these trans-actions, we could see the history of our tiny village play out before our eyes—at least, until my jet-lagged eyes started to glaze over. There were fifteen parcels in all for a total of 6.8 hectares—just over sixteen acres. Some of them were just a few hundred square meters. Soon I would learn the brilliant logic behind Stenberg's acquisitions. (Hint: it was all about the water.)

"So," Maître Bortolloti said once we had signed a stack of docu-ments in triplicate, "here are the keys."

He reached into a drawer and pulled out Ofilio's plastic bag and dumped them out on his desk. There must have been a hundred keys in all: old Victorian gate keys, mortise door keys with four-inch stems, ordinary padlock keys, a ring of keys I was told controlled the steel shutters on the upstairs windows, mechanically cut keys for the garage and the house, and an assortment of cabinet keys. There were keys for the cistern, keys to the pump house, keys to the pool room, keys for the cellar, keys for the tool room behind the tower, keys for the large wooden gates at the bottom of the 250-meter-long driveway, and keys to the wrought-iron gate in the stone archway that opened onto the house. Some of them were duplicates, some were unique, and few of them had labels. Ofilio must have started to

remove them as payback, then given up. It would take hours to figure out which opened what.

When we had finished and were saying our goodbyes, Jean-Jacques offered to buy us a drink, so we all went down to the port. He could have come right out of a Truffaut movie, a young Antoine Doinel (played by Jean-Pierre Léaud), whose brooding intensity could explode into wacky bursts of ecstasy. And he was ecstatic now, his arm draped around the shoulders of his fiancée, who pretended she did not notice as his hand slipped beneath her arm and into her bra from behind.

"You cannot believe the thievery of the French state, *monsieur*. I have been to this property maybe three times in my life. My mother used to come from New Caledonia to spend the summers, so when she died, it went to the three of us brothers. Just to get up to the house, you had to get that thief Ofilio—you met him, did you not?—to hire someone to cut the underbrush, and that cost a couple thousand euros. And so now we inherit it, and the French state wants half of it—half of it! And in cash! None of my brothers had any interest in the place, so Maryse and I prefer to take what we can get and start our life together. Here's to your health!"

Maryse was visibly shocked at his account of the rapacity of the French state.

"Half?" she said, tipping down her sunglasses to glare at him. "You never told me that."

In his manic relief at having pulled off the sale, Jean-Jacques didn't seem to notice this brief, dark note. We drank together for an hour or so, basking in the late-afternoon sun (the port of Saint-Tropez faces west, so it gets the last light of the day). I was  happy for the two of them. They would get married in a week and were planning to spend their "pre-honeymoon" at the Hôtel Sube just above us, overlooking the port, no doubt eating and drinking up a good portion of his inheritance. Would Maryse still want him when he was poor? Something told me she would not. But I had more pressing things to do than speculate on their relationship. I wanted to get back before sunset to prepare for my first night in our new house.

Sleeping with the Boar

Luxurious, it was not. Despite the warmth of the spring day, the house was cold and damp, so I opened the windows to let it air. Then I took stock of what Christina and I (and the French bank) now owned.

The kitchen was a disaster of dingy Formica; the stand-alone cabinets could have been secondhand when they were installed in the mid-1960s. Instead of countertops, a mahogany table gobbled up half the room. The walls and ceiling were painted sky blue, creating an aquarium effect that made you feel small and trapped. My task over the next three weeks was to wave the magic wand over it all.

The dining room was better. It had a high vaulted ceiling and whitewashed walls that were hung with copies of the Unicorn Tapestries. (We had visited a boutique in Carcassonne in the autumn that sold the same reproductions, so when Jean-Jacques tried to sell them to us at twice the price, I successfully negotiated him down.) A long peasant's table was surrounded by eight straight-backed caned chairs. There was also a buffet of dark oak, and built-in bookcases flanking a low cupboard. We paid Jean-Jacques an extra five thousand euros to buy the furniture. It wasn't our first choice, but it meant less work for me. We would replace what we wanted later.

But the galvanizing feature was a basalt plaque that looked like a gravestone, cemented into the far wall. The puzzling inscription read *goto frcaus avocatus*, with a Templar cross and a date—1099—in

Roman numerals. Along with the brick floors and the wrought-iron sconces and railings and a stone statue of the Virgin Mary set high in the staircase, the house had a monastic feel to it. This was further enhanced by statuary niches cut in the exterior walls. One of these niches, which faced the vineyards and the distant ocean, held

a time-eaten mosaic of an Etruscan woman's  face. I had seen the same face in Lebanon in the fortified palace of a Sunni warlord who boasted that he had plundered Carthage in the 1950s and taken away every tile of a mosaic-lined pool, recreating it beneath the cypresses of his estate overlooking Beirut.

Upstairs was the great room with its fifteen-foot ceiling supported by gigantic hand-hewn beams joined with wooden pegs. The centerpiece was a fireplace set in a mass of flat stones. On the far wall was a large painting of a Swedish forest at the end of winter, with delicate twilight spilling over hills and a distant lake, undoubtedly left over from Stenberg's time. The other end was all windows with an expansive view of vineyards, olive orchards, Sainte-Maxime, and the sea. I knew instantly that this was where I would write my books. French doors gave onto a large elevated terrace, which Véronique had called the "solarium," walled with stone pillars and wrought ironwork and surmounted on one side by thick glass panels to hold off the mistral. It had a 360-degree view of hills and valleys and mountains and

sea. I drank in the last rays of  the sun and treasured the rich perfume of the eucalyptus trees below. I was home.

As I was preparing my bed later on, I heard a weird scraping and huffing sound just below my window. Looking out, I saw three wild boars routing down by the pool as if they owned it. They didn't care in the least that someone was about. I needed to buy a hunting rifle, I thought. Just watching them made me hungry!

Cat Invasion

From the beginning of time, there have been cat people—feline and supple, thriving on subtleties—and there have been dog people. Christina and I were most resolutely dog people. And while she grew up with cats on the farm south of Stockholm—working cats that hunted mice in the barns—I didn't understand them one bit. To me, cats were an alien species. All that purring didn't fool me. They were hostiles.

The next morning, I found an odd wooden construction inside the enclosed veranda beneath the solarium. It contained two bowls: one for water, the second for dried cat food. If the cat nudged them, more water and food would drop down from containers inside. It had been left there by the Millots, who we learned from the ever-entrepreneurial Madame Bardot were regular renters from Paris who paid good money to stay in the house for six weeks during the summer. If we played our cards right, we could keep them and reduce our annual mortgage payments by nearly half. Not bad for just getting out of the way, I thought.

The Millots had left the sliding door to the veranda open a crack for the cat. When I opened it the first time, I nearly lost my lunch. The dank room, which still smelled of winter, was steeped in cat urine.

Now, if you are a dog person and have ever visited a cat person's house, you know what I mean about the odor. It *stank*. The urine plus the damp and the lack of fresh air called for a bucket of bleach. I tossed the wooden contraption out onto the pebbles and opened the sliding doors wide and avoided the place for days.

During that first week I was planning and bustling and building. I emailed Christina drawings for the kitchen, and we quickly decided on cabinets painted in distressed yellow and blue, the signature Provençal colors we had decided to make our central theme. The plan was to strip the room to the bare walls, repaint them a light yellow, and install new cabinets and wooden countertops and a five-burner gas range with a brass towel bar and a matching black hood. I was even planning to dig out the dirty wall tiles with their Betty Crocker illustrations and replace them with vast expanses of deep blue ceramics rimmed with a geometric motif and the occasional insert of olives or ripe peaches.

If we wanted to seriously rent out the house—not just to the summer Parisians—that was just the beginning. I also needed to buy outdoor furniture, new bedding, and household items and repaint the bathrooms. And *then* I had to talk to local real estate agents to find renters.

In the meantime, America had gone to war. Every morning I listened to the increasingly surreal reports on France Inter, the French national radio network. Foreign Minister Dominique Galouzeau de Villepin was not content to disagree with the United States, as did a certain number of our allies; he actively sought to rally world leaders and public opinion to treat the United States—not Saddam Hussein—as the enemy. As the battle to liberate Basra stretched on for days, French commentators began calling it the "martyred city"—not because Saddam had murdered so many of Basra's Shiite inhabitants, which he had, but because US and British troops had laid a careful siege to minimize the suffering of civilians, dragging out the war.

A poll came out showing that 25 percent of the French hoped Saddam would win the war. It got so bad that Prime Minister Jean-Pierre Raffarin reminded his fellow citizens that despite France's rejection of the US-led war, Saddam Hussein was the enemy, not America.

I encountered none of this hostility, however. One day, after spending hours at the Castorama in Toulon, I struck up a conversation with the kitchen consultant as he helped me load two shopping carts full of stuff into my rented Renault Laguna. He was in his mid-thirties, with straw-colored hair and as clean-cut as Tintin, a famous French cartoon character.

"I hear the war is going badly," he said.

"Actually, it's not," I said.

"That's what we hear on the radio."

"I know. And it's totally false. The Pentagon plan projected it would take three weeks to reach Baghdad. We're just in the middle of the second week."

"It's funny, we never hear about that," he said. "Don't worry, sir. *C'est de la foutaise*—it's just a crock—and everybody knows it. It's a pleasure to hear a bit of truth. That's why so many people in this country never listen to the news."

We were reaching the end of a brilliant sunny day, the kind of early spring day that drove Parisian weathermen to despair. "*La France est coupée en deux*," they would say, applying a shopworn formula about political division to the weather. The top half—the better half, they implied—was cold and rainy, but the south was bathed in sunshine. How unfair! The people of Provence had done nothing to deserve this. What an affront to the superior beings that inhabited Left Bank cafés! The salesman wished me well and went off to enjoy his evening.

We had loaded the Laguna until it sat low on the springs, so it was with some trepidation that I turned the key…and nothing. It was getting late and the store was closing, and I wondered if I had violated the fine print by overloading the car and had gotten caught. Luckily, the salesman was still there and called a tow truck, but I waited nearly an hour before it showed up. I limped home in the darkness, glad to finally make it.

I HAD SCHEDULED THREE WEEKS to complete the renovations, so I slept little and worked until 3:00 a.m. on the kitchen or other indoor projects. During the day, I took advantage of the good weather to clear brush and explore the hillside. And that was when I finally saw the cat.

I was working below the pool with a gas-powered brush cutter fitted with a *couteau à ronces*, a two-pronged blade with the ends folded over like winglets that allowed you to grind brush, not just cut it. You started at the top of a white- or pink-flowered *ciste* and worked down to the dirt, taking care not to hit the stones. Hitting the stones not only dulled the blades—you discarded them when they became flat—but created sparks. And in dry months, that could set fire to the hillside.

It was heavy going, and the turpentine bushes and heather were over ten feet high with trunks as thick as my wrist. I quickly realized I was going to need a bigger machine to tackle them, and when I turned around to head back up the hill, there was the cat, just staring at me as if I were the invader and it were at home.

It was a mangy white cat, thin and disheveled. Not the type of cat you would parade about on a leash or even want to hold in your lap. Patches of fur were missing around its neck and between its ears, either from mange or ripped out by some predator. And it had ghoulish pink eyes that matched the pink blotches of skin.

"Okay, cat," I said in French. "You win. You know where to get food and water. Now I will give you a bowl of milk."

I was drinking milk in my coffee then, so I had fresh milk on hand and set a bowl of it just outside the kitchen door and watched.

"Come on, cat. Drink the milk," I said in French again. After all, why would a French cat speak English?

You can see I didn't know anything about cats.

The cat just stared at me, ten or fifteen feet away, sinking into a crouch as if ready to pounce.

"If you don't want the milk, I can take it away," I said, and made to pick up the bowl and remove it. The cat took two steps closer to me then, so I set down the milk in front of the kitchen window so I could watch from inside.

For several minutes, the cat just stood by the round terrace, ears alert, head flicking occasionally at some distant sound—or perhaps to make sure I wasn't trying to outsmart it. When it was sure I was not about to execute some secret diabolical plot, it approached, one step at a time, pausing, another step, pausing, until finally it reached the bowl and dipped in a paw.

Dipped in a paw! I couldn't believe it. I thought cats were supposed to be superclean, and this cat was putting his paw into his milk? And then, of course, he licked his paw, as if perhaps the poison I had put in the milk to lure him to his death would be less powerful if first diluted by fur.

This ballet went on for several days as I learned new trades. Our kitchen design called for me to install the range on the inner wall, where it would stand directly beneath the chimney I had discovered while examining the 2,500-liter cistern in the crawl space above the kitchen. I bought a propane torch and solder and copper tubing and tube anchors and learned how to move the gas line to where it needed to be. Next, I ripped out most of the electricity and used a grinder to cut channels into the cement and plaster walls for new wiring tubes. I was having difficulty removing the wall tiles, so in some places I decided to tile over them and had to apply a layer of leveling cement to keep the surface flat.

Installing the upper cabinets went much smoother than I had feared. When I'd renovated the kitchen in our Victorian house in Kensington, Maryland, I'd had to cope with hundred-year-old lathing and crumbling plaster, so sinking anchors was a challenge. Here, I had an inch and a half of cement before hollow brick, so even if I drilled through to the brick, the screw anchors had plenty of material to grip.

In the evenings I would set out a bowl of fresh milk, and in the mornings it would always be empty. When the cat allowed me to see it, which was not often, it appeared to be gaining weight, so one day when I was shopping I bought a few cans of solid cat food, liver and chicken or whatever it was that cats were supposed to like.

The first time I opened the can of liver I could hear the cat. It was actually meowing from somewhere beyond the terrace.

"Ah, so you like that, little cat," I said in French.

"Meow," said the cat, also in French.

"I hope you know how to hunt mice," I said.

"Meow," said the cat.

With this, I thought we had come to terms.

But I was wrong. A cat knows a dog person when it sees one, and there is no peace to be made. "I am the cat who walks by himself, and all places are alike to me," wrote Kipling in a *Jungle Book* story I used to read to our children. I soon learned exactly what that meant. One evening, when the cat had eaten and was purring and seemed to be contentedly falling asleep on the round terrace, I slowly approached and tried to pick it up. Instead of letting me stroke it, it put out its claws and scratched my arm from the elbow to the wrist.

"That's it, cat," I said. "You can go back to hunting mice. No more food for you."

Bay of Pigs

Some days were just too beautiful to spend indoors, so I took to exploring the hillside. I bushwhacked up to the cistern, following the tunnels carved out by the wild boar through the ten-foot-high brush, certain there must be a shorter path than the road we had taken with Ofilio. As I stood on the edge of the cistern looking down at the house, about a kilometer below, I thought I saw what looked like a ridgeline in the underbrush. I followed it as far as I could, then got down on hands and knees to clear a way through the Scotch broom and the giant heather. Once I had determined the right direction for the path, I came back with the brush saw and widened it.

Our Swedish friends in Beauvallon had a French gardener who came by once or twice a month. Bruno wasn't really a gardener; he was an off-duty gendarme who worked in Saint-Tropez. Christina thought he would be perfect to cut back the mimosa below the house that was blocking our view of the valley. Bruno was good-natured and never complained. He came originally from Marseille and spoke the thick local *patois* the northerners joked they could stir with a spoon. One morning he came chugging up our driveway in his ancient Renault 4, a relic from the *gendarmerie* a generation ago. I told him what I wanted done, and without question, he set to work.

Two days later, I realized I should have supervised him more closely. I couldn't see him from the kitchen window, but every now and then, I saw him taking a break, drenched in sweat. He was decapitating the trees with a pruning saw. Instead of a dense mass of green and yellow, we now had an army of chest-high stumps, headless and gray, frozen upright while on the march. It was a massacre.

"*Alors, ça vous plaît*, monsieur?" he said, proud of his work.

I didn't have the heart to say no. What he lacked in intelligence, he more than made up for in loyalty. The mimosa would grow back soon enough.

I MET THIERRY THROUGH ALEXIS, one of the neighbors we had gotten to know through the Swedes in Beauvallon. Thierry was the caretaker of Alexis's house and serviced the pool; he also did excavation and grading work with a small bulldozer. He stopped by from time to time in his gigantic Toyota Land Cruiser to see how I was doing, and we would chat and drink wine.

Thierry was the son of a well-known medical doctor and university professor. Early on, he determined he didn't want to become an intellectual like his father, so at the age of twenty, he got married and went off with his new wife, Chantal, to become a peasant. They left Aubagne, a city just outside of Marseille that was home to the Foreign Legion, and rented a small farm in the wilderness of the Ardèche.

People think of France as a vast civilized playground, from the green pastures of Normandy to the cafés of Paris and the beaches of Saint-Tropez. But that's because they've never been to the Ardèche. It was buried in the Massif Central, the high, rocky plateau lodged in the center of France like an axe buried in a four-hundred-year-old oak. It snowed so much in the winters that it blocked the roads and was so remote that no one ever came to plow them. They had two children during those winters. With their meager savings, they bought a few cows and goats and lived off the cheese and meat they produced. But as their children started to grow, the snow and the cold and the lack of running water lost its charm, and they wound up here, where Chantal had family. Thierry worked for a landscape gardener before starting his own business. He despised the crassness of the local tradesmen in Sainte-Maxime and Saint-Tropez, who were more interested in money than the quality of their work. There was an authenticity to Thierry and an inquisitiveness beneath his peasant exterior that I found appealing.

One afternoon after a few glasses of wine, I said I wanted to show him the cistern, so we grabbed gloves and branch cutters and headed up the hillside.

"Ha! You've worked well," he said once we had reached the cistern on my new path. "So, now where are these famous springs of Angélus?"

"That's what I'd like to find out."

He surveyed the hillside above us, where giant rocks stood out from the massive green carpet of the maquis. "If you ask me, it should be there."

The way beyond the cistern was completely overgrown. We emerged on a ridge that traversed the hillside along a fold in the landscape, with broad views of the house and the twisting *route départementale* down below and the rocky face of Hard Glue Mountain above.

"That's the ravine," Thierry said, pointing to the giant rocks we had seen from down below. "Follow it upward and you can see cane. It only grows around water. Your springs are nearby."

The going was a bit easier on this part of the road. The ground was rocky, and we could see the stain of water trickling down the stones, as if the earth itself was sweating. When we reached the ravine, it was completely overgrown with vines and thick grass, but we could hear the unmistakable sound of a waterfall. I stepped into the grass and wound up in water to my ankles. Thierry laughed good-naturedly.

"*Et voila de l'eau,*" he said. "As I told you."

He broke off a dead branch and began poking around until he found stones that he used to get closer to the waterfall, and then he parted the vines. There before us was a pool of water, perhaps twenty feet wide, carved out of rock, with a stream tumbling into it from the ravine above.

"Is this the spring?" I asked him.

"It's too open. It'll be mostly gone in the summer. The springs are not far. This is where the wild boar take their bath."

He loved the wild boar and talked about them often. As soon as I had told him about seeing the boar by our swimming pool, he'd asked what I wanted to do about it. He was delighted when I suggested shooting them.

"We will call this place La Baie des Cochons—the Bay of Pigs," I said.

"*La Baie des Cochons. Et bien*! That sounds like something American."

I laughed. "Cuban, actually. That's where Kennedy pulled the plug on the Cuban revolutionaries who were going to overthrow Castro."

"Ha. I always thought it was where hundreds of Americans were massacred."

"No, just Cubans."

"So you let others do the dying for you."

French is a more logical language than English, and words often call out for a certain response, as they did here. But I could tell he was just playing.

"Sure," I said. "Wouldn't you?"

"Especially when it comes to the wild pigs. I would like them to die right here." He raised his arms as if sighting a rifle. "Pang!"

As we walked back toward the cistern, Thierry stopped and listened. "I'll bet the springhead is just up there. If you will allow me, I will look around when I have time after you are gone."

"Absolutely," I said.

I was happy to have made a friend and knew that Thierry had a lot to teach me.

When we got back to the house, I pointed down to the swimming pool. It was so full of dead leaves that the water was almost black.

"You know what Ofilio told me? He said he drained the pool at the beginning of summer in order to clean it."

"*Et quoi encore!*" Thierry said. "What an idiot."

"The pool holds almost exactly the same amount of water as the cistern: thirty thousand liters. So no wonder he keeps telling me we need to drill a well. He uses up all our water refilling the pool right at the beginning of the dry season."

We struck a deal for Thierry to take over the pool, getting it cleaned and in working order for when we came back at the end of June—or earlier, if we managed to get renters.

Les Mandarines

One morning, the temperature dropped almost to freezing, but the sun was so bright and the sky such a deep blue that I went outside in shorts and T-shirt and felt invigorated. I decided to go for a jog and explore the *route départementale* that led to the pass and dropped down on the other side to the vineyards of Vidauban.

The road was not particularly steep at first, but it climbed steadily, and the landscape was dramatic and wild. After a few turns, there wasn't a house in sight. Way down below, the morning sun turned the water beyond Sainte-Maxime into quicksilver, so intense it burned the eyes to look at it. Powerful waterfalls rushed down the ravines and flowed beneath the roadway at virtually every turn. Although Provence is known as a semiarid climate where a cloudy day in summertime is an event, the road here was built to withstand tremendous powers of water, with thick cement bridges across the ravines.

As I came back down from the top, the view stretched out before me, and I was struck by a feeling that I had been here before. The whole area was deeply familiar, but until now I hadn't been able to figure out why that was. Then I saw the ochre-colored villa not five hundred meters above our house. Because of the curve and the angle and the trees sheltering the house, I hadn't noticed it on the way up. It was called Les Mandarines. We had driven by it ten years earlier, before we had moved to the States, and were so taken by the landscape and the view and the For Sale sign out front that I wrote down the number of the agent and called them the same day to send a brochure for the property.

By that point, we were packing up our house in Maisons-Laffitte and preparing to move to Maryland. Christina was not at all sure she wanted to leave France, so we were considering taking the money from the sale of Maisons-Laffitte and buying property in Provence. It all started coming back to me. The owners had wanted the exact same price for that four-bedroom villa, perched along the road with almost no land, as we paid ten years later for Angelus Springs with our sixteen acres of hillside! At the time, we thought it was outrageously expensive. Ten years later, it was a steal.

How much of our lives do we really control, and how much is in God's hands? Sometimes his guidance is blatant, but other times, it's not.

I am a strong believer in the power of the human will. Many years spent among Muslims in the Middle East has convinced me of the debilitating impact of blind fatalism. But there is a huge difference between shrugging your shoulders as you march out in front of rush hour traffic, saying your life is in Allah's hands, and dodging the oncoming cars. I believe God wants us to dodge the traffic.

I also believe that God at times leads us to paths where we fear we cannot possibly survive, only to guide us to safety by faith and the intervention of his angels. In that distinction lies the difference between fatalism and trust in God's goodness, Islam and Christianity. God does not want us to cower in the Valley of the Shadow of Death but to get across it as quickly as possible.

Asterix and Obelix

One late afternoon in the brilliant sunshine, I resumed my hunt for the springs. This time I started at the cistern. A stream of water was tumbling down the rocks across the road, so I followed it up into the brush. Straddling the rocks, I was able to cut the oily cistus and the heather near the root and toss them into the channel. The Scotch broom was more difficult because the thorns invariably got the better of my gloves. After twenty minutes or so, the water disappeared, and so I followed a boar run, cut like a tunnel into the undergrowth, until it emptied out onto a plateau up above. Although I was just a hundred yards or so above the cistern, this flat, open area was completely hidden by the steepness of the hillside and the surrounding brush. In the distance down below, I could see the house.

So where were the springs? Several hundred meters ahead, I could see the cane break above the Bay of Pigs. But I couldn't hear water— just the faint crackling the sun makes as it dries the leaves.

And then, all of a sudden, there it was: a black PVC pipe about two inches in diameter, sticking up out of the ground. Clearly, it was meant to carry water from the springs down to the cistern, but someone had sawed it cleanly in two. I was stunned. Why would anyone commit such an unprovoked act of vandalism? And how would they know where to look for the water pipe in the first place in the midst of the unbroken maquis?

The other end of the pipe lay about a foot away, and as I lifted it up, I saw that the ground beneath it was damp. A steady trickle of water was coming from it. So I started following the pipe as it plunged into the dense undergrowth, carefully cutting away the brush for about an hour until the sun disappeared and I had to head back down the mountain. There were so many steep drop-offs and stone terracing walls hidden by the brush that it would be treacherous to get lost in the dark. Whoever had cut the pipe knew the mountain well.

When I reached Lookout Rock, I saw Thierry's Land Cruiser parked down by my garage, along with another 4x4 I didn't recognize. It was another five minutes to get back to the house, so I broke into a jog so not to miss them.

"*Alors, l'américain,*" he said in greeting. "I was afraid maybe you had left already."

"No, I had to change my ticket to stay another week."

"I'm not surprised. You may have to change it again."

Thierry introduced the two friends he had brought over for me to meet. They were fellow tradesmen. Bastian was a plasterer who also did cement work. He was helping our friend Albert renovate his house down in the village next to the bakery. Marcel was born and raised here on the hillside and did stonework and brush clearing. He lived in the village along with his wife, who worked part-time cleaning houses. I was happy to get to know them; you never knew what type of services you might need, and I appreciated Thierry introducing me to people he trusted. I offered to get a bottle of rosé from the fridge, but I could see that didn't suit them.

"You wouldn't, uh, happen to have pastis?" Bastian said, expectantly.

"Surely even this American must have pastis," Thierry said with a laugh.

Rosé wine was not a "man's" drink, apparently. So I went inside and found glasses, ice cubes, pastis, and a carafe of water. I had learned the ritual of serving the anisette aperitif years before and so first put the ice cubes into the glasses, then poured the pastis, and then allowed my guests to serve themselves water to turn it milky. An old French joke from the days before sewage plants warned you not to drink water. *Look what it does to pastis!*

As we lit into our second round, I found out that the real reason they had come was for the wild boar. All three were avid hunters, or so they claimed, and my property was well known as a safe haven for the beasts.

"One day, when I was up on the hillside with my father, we saw three giant boar coming out of the ravine," Marcel said. "They must have weighed a hundred kilos each."

"But you didn't shoot them, did you?" Bastian said.

"What do you think? We were taking care of the tomatoes, not hunting."

"Even a gardener should always carry a gun," Bastian said. "You never know when you'll stumble across a pig who can shoot."

"Pigs can't shoot," Marcel said, quite seriously.

"Are you sure?"

"How could they hold a gun?"

"With their teeth."

Marcel and Bastian kept at it, and it became almost comical. Bastian was the shorter of the two, had quick eyes and a quick wit, and took pleasure in goading his friend. Marcel was large and chunky and fell into every trap that Bastian set. Later, Thierry told me he called them Asterix and Obelix, and it fit them perfectly. In the famous comic strip, Asterix is the short, wily Gaul who outwits the Romans, while Obelix tags along with a giant club and is more preoccupied with filling his stomach than killing centurions. And of course, their feast of preference is wild boar. Obelix frequently munches on an entire haunch of the beast, sinking into a fatuous contentment. I could see Marcel doing the same.

As they were getting ready to go, I told them about the cut water pipe.

"Who else but Ofilio could have done that?" I wondered. "It looks like it was freshly sawed off."

"Oh, you never know," Thierry said. "There are a lot more people than you would think prowling the hillside."

"Then what's the message?" I asked.

Marcel seemed to plunge into thought, and it made him look uncomfortable.

"*Aller, Marcel.* Don't tell us *you* did it?" Bastian said.

"No, no, of course not," he said quickly. "But when my father had his tomatoes up on the hillside, there was always water from the springs. Maybe this one just went dry."

"I doubt it," Thierry said. "These Americans are rich! They have water. They have wild pigs. They even have olives!" he said.

I could see he wasn't joking, and I was surprised.

"Olives?" I said.

"Yes, of course. Haven't you seen? The whole terrace below the pool is full of olive trees."

All I could see below the pool was a mass of dense foliage, a four-acre carpet woven with various shades of green. Christina and I had initially planned to buy a vineyard near Pierrefeu and grow enough grapes to pay the mortgage, but the economics weren't right. We had never thought about olive trees.

"What do you do with olives?" I asked.

"Why, you make oil, of course! The oil from Alexis's place is famous."

He nodded vaguely toward the neighbor's property across the valley. We had met Alexis just before Christmas through our Swedish friends. He was a dentist up in Paris but came down here several times a year, always bringing a different girlfriend to dally with him beside his heart-shaped pool and the two palm trees he had planted behind it. Thierry was right; now that I thought about it, Alexis had talked about his olive oil, although he had never offered to let us taste it.

"You'd have to clear the underbrush first. And then start pruning the trees. But if you work hard, you could get oil in two or three years."

I started to dream. Olive trees were symbols of the Pax Romana that had transformed the Mediterranean into a lake of commerce for eight hundred years. Because they took so long to cultivate, they only thrived in regions at peace. It is said that in some places in Italy and Spain, you could still find two-thousand-year-old trees that had first borne fruit at the time of Jesus. Here was yet another gift from God, hidden wealth neither I nor apparently the previous owners had suspected we had. Marcel cut into my reverie.

"You'd have to do it professionally," he said. "Do you have someone to clear your brush?"

"You mean besides that crook, Ofilio?"

"*Mais non, mais non,*" Thierry said. "He's not a crook. He's just a *fainéant.*" A lazy good-for-nothing. "He's Corsican. Didn't you know?"

"*Et alors?*" I said. I had spent many summers in Corsica and always found the French jokes about the laziness of the Corsicans missed the point. The Corsicans hated the French because they wanted to be free and rarely deigned to lift a finger for them. Their "laziness" was more a political statement than a character trait. Amongst themselves they could be quite energetic, indeed, especially when it came to land disputes, politics, and future sons-in-law. The bodies of Corsicans killed during these animated discussions littered the hills.

I asked Marcel if he could stop by during the daytime and have a look at the terrace and eventually give me an estimate. I had a lot to do before I started clearing all that brush, I said. But olive trees? Yes, I was interested.

I Will Cut It Off

When we discussed this new information over the phone the next day, Christina made it clear she wanted nothing to do with olive trees. "I've got a farm," she said. "That's enough to worry about." Her father had recently been diagnosed with prostate cancer, and although he was just eighty, she was certain he would be dead before the end of the year, leaving her and her sister to manage the 1,500-acre family farm in Sweden along with their dysfunctional brother.

Christina had never wanted to be a farmer and kept leaving home as a teenager to live as a boarder in nearby Södertälje and, later, Stockholm, where she attended better schools than those available in the countryside. Although Gnesta was just an hour south of Stockholm by train, it was another universe when she was growing up in the 1950s and 1960s. For one thing, there were no school buses, so in the wintertime she trudged through the snow on cross-country skis nearly two kilometers each way to school. (She has hated cross-country skiing ever since.) And then, there was no high school. The farm itself was a self-contained world. Every morning at precisely 7:00 a.m., her father, Ingemar, would ring the bell at the main barn, calling the thirty-three farmhands to assembly so he could dole out tasks for that day. He used to drive around to supervise them on a small red tractor. Behind his back, the farmhands called him "the Red Devil."

"That was in the late forties and early fifties, before industrialization," Christina said.

Whether they were plowing, sowing grain, installing drainage pipes, thinning the forests, logging, or repairing one of the forty-two roofs on the property (many of them small cottages where the laborers lived with their families), Ingemar knew where everyone was supposed to be at every moment of the day and regularly checked up on them. Later, of course, he took out loans and bought tractors and a harvester, and toward the end he was managing the entire farm with just two other people and a forestry cooperative. But it was constant work. Growing up with her father's seemingly boundless energy and ability to get things done, she naturally assumed that all men—at least, all men worth her time—should work as hard and be as productive. Did I mention that Ingemar and I shared the same birthday, November 4? I only found that out after we got married.

After college, Christina went to work for the Swedish Ministry of Industry. She married her college sweetheart, who was the son of a famous former ambassador. After several years they had a son and soon afterward got divorced. Her main complaint was that her husband was too diplomatic, never spoke his feelings, and gave into her whims rather than openly oppose them. "He never would say what he really wanted," she said once.

The minister of industry—her ultimate boss—had a habit of dropping by her tiny office or stopping her in the corridor to chat. Christina didn't think anything about it, an attitude that amused her colleagues. One afternoon, he called and offered to take her to dinner, knowing that she was single again. "He had a reputation for flirting, so I just politely told him no," she said. The minister's advance, of course, would be considered sexual harassment in the United States, except that there was no harassment and no retaliation for Christina's refusal. Having seen Christina put her foot down, I can understand why he left her alone. When she is determined not to do something, she is like a horse that digs all four hooves into the ground. You could rope her and hog-tie her, but you couldn't budge her.

She and Anders divorced amicably when Niclas was just four. After a year of shared custody, she decided to put her government career on hold, leave Niclas behind, and take a job with the OECD in Paris. She had seen her mother's horizons cut short by her willingness to put duty as a farmer's wife before self-fulfillment and was determined not to sacrifice her own dreams for the sake of a lifeless marriage. So she decided to act out a love of France she had learned from a high school French teacher.

Now, in truth, it wasn't hard to fall in love with Paris in the early 1980s, especially if you were single. This was before the AIDS epidemic made responsible adults more cautious about sex with strangers. Paris was enchanted, where a new adventure lurked just around the corner and yesterday's fling was soon forgotten, and Christina took full advantage of the freedoms Paris offered. That is, until she met me. "I never thought I'd get married again," she said later. "I didn't come to Paris to look for a husband but to get away from one!"

By this point, I had two children, had separated from their mother, and lost an agonizing custody battle, mainly because I was American and she was French and we were not married. I had met another French woman I intended to marry; we had even set the date, put down a deposit on the wedding hall, sent out invitations, and found a house we wanted to buy in Triel-sur-Seine, outside of Paris. But then I met Christina and my world turned upside down—or right-side up, as it turned out. My life of casual relationships without consequences was about to end.

At first, Christina pretended shock when I announced I had canceled my wedding plans.

"I had nothing to do with that," she insisted.

"You had everything to do with that," I said.

"It was just sex."

"But you liked it."

She smiled and gave one of her Swedish singsong answers, a long, drawn-out "ahh" that sounded like a three-note phrase played on a slide flute.

Then she ran away from me—literally. Just as we were starting to develop a relationship, without warning she left Paris for Washington to visit a Japanese woman she had met at the OECD. "I wanted to see if I missed you," she said later. From then on, we fell deeper in love and decided to bring our families together. We married before the law in Stockholm in April; then in June, we had a religious service at the American Church in Paris. It was pouring cats and dogs when it came time for the reception, which we planned to hold in the magnificent Bagatelle gardens in the Bois de Boulogne. Instead, we herded our guests into a renovated stable and drank champagne cocktails called *pêchers*. Similar to a kir, but with a dash of peach liquor, it was a play on the French word for sin. Julian and Niclas, who were eight and nine years old respectively, were dressed all in white and raced each other through the mud outside until their trousers turned brown. Christina said the rain was a good omen.

"It means we will have good fortune," she said. "It is raining money."

That was good news to me, since I had been so poor when I first came to Paris in the mid-1970s that the soles of my shoes flopped in the rain. There were many mornings when I didn't know how I would eat that night.

Not long after the wedding in Paris, we went with my brother and friends for couscous in the Quartier Latin. We drank bottle after bottle of dark Algerian wine, and people we didn't know seemed to melt into our party. At one point, I started chatting with a blonde-haired girl who spoke French with what I thought was a charming accent—until Christina came up from behind me and told me she was leaving. I said it was still early, we should have another bottle of wine with our new friends.

"I'm leaving *now*," she said, her face turned to stone despite all the wine. "If you want to stay with that Polish girl, that's it. It's finished. You can have her, or me."

So I jumped up and we took a cab home in silence. For three days, she didn't speak a word to me. She rolled away when I tried to approach her in bed. Finally, I came up behind her as she was trimming the fat from some meat in our tiny kitchen and put my head on her shoulder.

"I'll cut it off," she said, "if you ever do that again."

"What do you mean?"

"I'll cut it off so no one else can use it. I will cook it, too."

She smashed the big butcher's knife down hard on the cutting board, and instinctively I leapt backward. Six years later, when Lorena Bobbitt, a young Ecuadorian immigrant, cut off the member of her abusive husband, Christina felt vindicated. "At least I didn't have to do it to you," she said. "But I will."

And she would. I had great respect for Christina's iron will and her indifference to the sight of blood. After all, she was brought up helping the vet deliver calves at the farm. Her mother used to take an axe and chop the heads off live chickens.

Every now and then, Christina gave a little demonstration of her sangfroid, just to remind me to stay on my good behavior. One summer, when Simon was playing in the dollhouse on the farm in Sweden—he was just a year and a half—she saw a poisonous snake called an *orm* slither between the stones just underneath. She ran out and grabbed Simon. Then she put on rubber boots and found a spade and waited for nearly an hour until the snake stuck its head up again. She chopped it off with a single blow.

It's one thing to be a Christian, which I was. It's quite another to keep the Lord's commandments. When I got married, I never imagined that I would be required to respect number seven, certainly not in France. (That's the one the Israelites sent Moses back up Mount Sinai to renegotiate.) There were days before I met Christina when literally I had one girl for breakfast, another one for lunch, and a third for dinner. Every street corner in Paris, every café, every museum, even the subway, seemed dedicated to the art of seduction. Women actually returned your glance—often with surprising candor—something that rarely happened in the US. Most creative people have a strong libido, and as a writer, I was no exception. Thanks to the threat of Christina's butcher knife, I learned to channel that energy into productive projects.

And yes, I can say with a straight face that I have kept that commandment, and in doing so, I discovered to my utter astonishment that I was much happier than I had ever been in the throes of debauchery. I could just be a father and not have to explain the presence of strange women in the house to my children. As my own faith deepened, I became grateful to Christina for helping me to understand that God's commandments were designed to keep us happy, armoring us against evil and self-destruction, and that adultery was the ultimate breach of trust, the ultimate lie. Faithfulness to her set me free.

What Real Men Do on Their Vacation

Even with the extra week, I worked down to the wire to finish the kitchen, plant the garden with flowers, repaint the bathrooms, and buy sheets and towels for eventual renters. As the kitchen took shape, it was vastly more attractive than I had imagined, and I realized the transformation from 1960s kitsch wouldn't be complete unless I replaced the conglomerate cement floor tiles as well. To gain time, I covered the old floor rather than break it, always making sure I had a dry section to walk on while I did other work.

As I was putting up the last wall tiles by the sink, I positioned my camera to commemorate the event. I had just finished dinner, washed down with a bottle of Côte du Rhône from Olivier Bernard, a large producer near Orange who always managed to bring out the red current, plum, and strawberry aromas in his viognier. Right behind me, the clock showed 2:30 a.m. I look a bit loopy in the photo in cement-specked T-shirt and shorts, rubber mallet, and latex gloves, leaning over the countertop to tap in the tile. I was leaving the next morning and still had one more section of floor tiles to do, but I needed to sleep.

Thierry answered my urgent call in the morning and came over to help clean up so I wouldn't miss my plane. I had just placed the last floor tile when he arrived. The wet saw was outside, tools were everywhere, and I had fifteen minutes to wash, lock the house, and drive. I started jogging from task to task, my heart pumping with adrenaline,

dismantling the workbench and hauling it to the tool room, washing the kitchen table, folding sheets from the clothesline behind the
tower. For a minute or two, he just watched me in amusement, arms
folded across his chest, without saying a word. I must have jogged
past him two or three times and was pouring with sweat.

"*Allez*, leave all that," he said finally. "Go wash so you don't frighten
the tourists."

"*Ces Amérloques*," he would say later when telling this story, using
a colloquialism for my nationality. "Pedal to the metal, racing around
the world. Afghanistan, Iraq, le Var. Leaving in *catamini*—catastro-
phe—hoping their friends will clean up the mess."

But he was happy to be that friend, and I was happy to have him.
We became thick as thieves.

A few weeks later, I called him from Washington. To my growing dismay, I learned that the wild boar had routed through the new
flower beds, there had been little rain, and the weather was already
hot. "But the *Amérloques* don't have to worry about water. You are
rich! I have found your spring," he said.

One afternoon after taking care of the pool, he had bushwhacked above the cistern, tracking the pipe I had found. He followed it along one of the old stone walls that delimited the landholdings; then it looped around a waterfall and up a steep boar track until it reached the cane break about a hundred meters above the Bay of Pigs. There, he found two black pipes sticking up out of the ground, and they were flowing with water.

"I believe you have two springs, not one," he said.

I didn't know what a spring was supposed to look like and was a bit underwhelmed.

"That's all there is? A couple of plastic pipes?"

"Wait," he said. "One of them is buried, so I think the spring is close. The other goes farther up the ravine where I found the basin."

The catch basin was a cement box cast around a cleft of the rock, three inches thick. The lid took all his strength to slide back and revealed an opening five feet by two feet full of cold water.

"There must have been a road up here before," he said. "No one could have hauled that much cement up here by hand."

I was excited, eager to explore on my own. Although my next book was titled *The French Betrayal of America* and would tell the story of Chirac and Villepin's perfidious undoing of the two-hundred-year alliance between our two countries, I was in love with France as much as ever. Besides, as Madame Bardot liked to remind me, the hostility toward America shown by France's current leaders was just politics, anyway. Politics and big money.

I ARRIVED A FEW DAYS AHEAD of Christina and the children at the end of June for our first vacation together at our new house. Christina had taken a half dozen white tiles and painted them in blue and yellow with the name of the house—Les Sources d'Angélus. I glued them onto a rectangular piece of wood and fitted the back with hooks so we could hang it from the stone pillars at the bottom of our driveway. Thierry came by for the christening, and we popped a bottle of the local bubbly in celebration. Although the dirt road leading to our gates was public, I had yet to meet anyone on it, so the sign was basically for us, the renters, and the woman who delivered the mail.

Christina walked through the yard with a pair of branch cutters, snipping here and there, parting larger branches by hand, giving me orders which trees to cut to open up the view.

"But the view *is* open," I protested.

I come from a culture where you're not supposed to cut trees. Christina comes from a culture where trees are a crop. She knows how fast they grow, and how quickly they become a nuisance. Where I see a bush bristling with foliage, little more than a bump, she sees a fully mature cork oak growing to thirty meters or more. And they are everywhere on our hillside. "It's easier to cut them when they are still young," she said.

We ate simple lunches of tomatoes and avocados, sliced country ham, cheese, and fresh fruit at the round terrace sheltered beneath four giant cork oaks, overlooking the pool and the olive orchards and vineyards and the Mediterranean beyond. The sky was a deep blue, and for the first week, there was hardly any wind, much to the chagrin of Diana and Simon, who we drove down to Saint-Maxime after lunch for sailing class. We bought kegs of the local rosé from the Cave des Maures in the village and bottled it ourselves. They called it Rêve d'Eté, and it was as pale and delicate as a summer afternoon dream and all too easy to drink.

I installed spotlights in the garden, transforming the yard from a spooky, foreboding place where wild animals lurked into an enclave of civilization. At night, we grilled meat and ate outside, often with friends, and the cicadas were so loud you had to shout over them. The cicadas' song is like a symphony, complex and microtonal, with a whole orchestra of instruments spread across the hillside. Occasionally their hidden conductor tunes them to perfect synchrony and they become a single harmonious chant. But invariably they break into contrapuntal discord, tearing against each other—until without warning they just stop, and never at the same hour of the evening. From *allegro con brio* the rhythm slows and the players walk off the stage one by one until the last lone cicada closes the show. The sudden stillness always came as a surprise. Sounds gradually emerged from the hillside we couldn't hear before: a distant dog barking, a car downshifting on the other side of the valley, the occasional hoot of an owl, the swish of a bat. Our peaceable kingdom.

In the mornings before it got too hot, I headed up the mountain with my brush cutter to extend the paths up to the springs. The going was not easy. The terrain was steep, strewn with rocks, and the heather had grown so thick in spots that I had to saw through it on hands and knees. By the time I got back to the house for lunch, my hair was matted, my arms were covered with scratches from the Scotch broom, and my blue jeans were heavy with sweat. I marked the path up to the

cistern with small squares of white tile left over from the kitchen, and the path beyond it to the springs with blue. By the end of our stay, I managed to clear a two-kilometer jogging trail, all on our own property. I called one section Paradise South, because it reminded me of the backcountry terrain at Mad River Glen where I had learned to ski as a teenager. I even carved the name into a wooden board and hung it from a cork oak at the top. It plunged down from rock to rock, then suddenly turned and plunged again. Whether climbing up or jogging down, it gave you thigh burn.

ONE EVENING OUR SWEDISH FRIENDS from Beauvallon came by. The mistral was howling, whipsawing the eucalyptus trees, banging at shutters we had forgotten to fasten. The wind was so fierce and so constant you were just waiting for something to crash. It was then that we discovered yet another example of Stenberg's genius.

We had been wondering why he had built an enclosed veranda beneath the solarium that could only be accessed from the outside. It

had giant windows on three sides and a panoramic view of the sea. At the back was a small fountain built of the same classic mosaic tiles as the pool. During normal evenings it was hot and stuffy, but with the mistral it was protected, calm, and yet fully integrated into the violent landscape. We lit it up like a cathedral with candles on the stone ledges. That's when we dubbed it the "mistral room."

Harold and Lise were way too fortunate for their own good. Their fathers were brothers, but because they were ambassadors in the Swedish foreign service in faraway countries, they only got to know each other as teenagers during summer holidays back home. When they fell in love, they required a dispensation from the government to get married because of the close blood tie. Harold spent his early years as a copywriter for an advertising agency in southern Sweden. Then an aunt died, left him money, and he decided he was an artist. So they moved to Provence, where he painted large, garish landscapes that he hung in their living room and never worked another day of his life. Christina had known Harold since college.

"Why aren't you down at the beach?" Lise asked me, when I told her about my mornings cutting brush. "Why don't you just hire somebody to do that?"

I shrugged. "I enjoy it," I said.

"It's what real men do on their vacation," Christina said. And then she just laughed, as if astonished to realize the implicit slight at Lise's husband. The two of them joined her in uproarious hilarity, as if it was the funniest thing they had ever heard.

As much as I loved Harold, he was no artist. But he bore no grudges and enjoyed a good joke. Besides, both of them knew that Christina had a much larger brush saw at her farm in Sweden, where she regularly culled young birch and beech and hemlock from the slow-maturing commercial forest of *tall*—the Swedish version of Scotch pine.

The conversation turned to our children, and Lise sighed that their oldest son was struggling in school in Stockholm. We remarked how much Diana and Simon had learned by attending the local French schools the previous autumn. Maybe they should put him in school in Sainte-Maxime?

"What? Here?" Lise exclaimed. She was truly shocked. "I would never dream of letting my children go to school here."

"Why not?" I asked. "We thought the *collège* where Diana went was pretty good."

In French, *collège* is the equivalent of junior high school.

"I don't want *my* son going to school with the son of the gardener," she said indignantly.

Christina and I just looked at each other, a bit taken aback.

"I can't imagine any better place for them to go," I said finally. "The gardener probably knows more that is of use than all the professors up in Paris."

"If we move back to France, it's going to be Neuilly, where at least he'll have friends who are the sons of ambassadors and aristocrats," she said.

I was thinking I would rather my kids went to school with the son of the gardener than with the sons of wannabe artists and aristocrats who haven't worked in twenty years or produced anything of substance with their leisure. And you never knew—the gardener's son might grow up to become president one day.

But I bit my tongue.

Fire!

We returned to the States after the Fourth of July, so I was back in Kensington when I received a phone call from Bruno, the gendarme-cum-gardener, on the twenty-ninth. It was not like him to make an international call, so I was surprised. These were the days when international phone calls were still expensive.

"Monsieur, monsieur!" he shouted, breathless.

"What's happening, Bruno?"

"Monsieur, there has been *une incendie*—a fire. A big fire. The whole hillside has burned."

One of our fears when we bought the house was that it quite literally would go up in smoke. It was well known that arsonists set fires at the onset of the mistral, knowing the wind could turn a small blaze into an uncontainable monster in minutes. Sometimes the arsonists got caught, but usually their names were redacted by the media. It was rumored that some of them were firefighters, seeking to augment their pay. Others were said to be real estate speculators, hoping to snatch up condemned property on the cheap. In the old days, when the hillsides were still cultivated by farmers and work animals, they would call in a fire master to set a controlled blaze to clear an overgrown area for cultivation. The master knew from the wind exactly where to set the fire and where it would turn and where to cut fire breaks to keep it under control.

"Are the Millots okay?" I asked. These were the renters from Paris.

"I haven't seen them," Bruno said. "The fire came down to the village and then turned and went back up toward Vallaury. It's total chaos. Half of Sainte-Maxime has evacuated. Three firefighters were trapped in their vehicles when the wind changed and were killed."

I had a moment of horror at the thought the Millots might have been trapped like those firefighters. What were you supposed to do in a fire? I had vague images of filling bathtubs and stuffing wet towels under doorways and instructions to close all shutters and stay as close to the ground as possible. If you had time, you were supposed to turn off gas bottles or dump them in the swimming pool if you had one. Worst of all was to try to flee. In most cases, a wind-driven fire would pass over the house so quickly, jumping from treetop to treetop, that in a few minutes, it would be gone.

As soon as I got off with Bruno, I tried to telephone the house, and then Monsieur Millot's cell phone, but neither one answered. Then I tried Thierry, but his phone didn't answer either. I called Christina in Sweden and explained what had happened.

"They must have cut the phones and the electricity," she said.

We could only wait, and pray.

The praying part became increasingly important as I read accounts of the deadly fire on the internet. It had started in midafternoon outside Vidauban, in the dense forest on the other side of our mountain. The local news reports claimed it had been set by the same arsonist who had set fire to an area closer to the town of Vidauban itself just two weeks earlier. How they knew that was anyone's guess. But the devastation was enormous. The firefighters tried to stop it using Canadair tankers that would take on water in the Gulf of Saint-Tropez and drop it at the fire head, but they quickly gave up and let it burn. There were few houses on that side of the mountain, and as they explained later, their goal was to save towns and villages and as many houses as possible, not the wilderness.

But as I learned later that afternoon on another call with Bruno, the winds were so strong that the fire raced up the mountain and crossed over the top and then burned the entire hillside above our property. The wind was driving it toward the east, toward the sea, so instead of plunging downward to us, it ran along the ridgeline and turned downward on the hillside across from us where our neighbor Alexis lived, continuing to follow the ridge as it curved around. Apparently, it had passed over our property entirely.

I phoned Alexis, and unlike the others, he picked up.

"Are you okay?" I asked him.

Alexis had bought a run-down sheep farm thirty years earlier from the co-owner of the *Nouvel Observateur*, a liberal newsweekly in Paris. He renovated the large one-room house, turning it into a *garçonnière*—a suggestive term for a bachelor's pad—using old brass plumbing fixtures and soapstone sinks and built-in cabinets with armoire doors he bought at flea markets. The bedroom was an immense loft that looked down onto a walk-in fireplace that filled the house with smoke whenever it was windy. Below the house he had planted an olive grove using only the *petit ribier* varietal and bragged about its superior qualities, but in truth, he had selected it because it was the only one he could get cheap and in quantity at the time.

"I'm in a hotel in Juan-les-Pins with a girl," he said, laughing.

"What about your house?"

"I have no idea," he said. "I can't reach Thierry or Bastian or Albert." These were our three mutual friends in the village.

"I can't either," I said.

I conveyed what I had learned from Bruno the gardener.

"It doesn't look good," he agreed. "Sh-shh!" he whispered, covering the phone. "Not now!"

"What's her name?" I asked.

"Estelle—I think. Hey, sweetheart. You're called Estelle, right?"

The next day I got an email from Monsieur Millot. He and his wife had evacuated to Sainte-Maxime at the first sign of smoke. When the fire turned in that direction, they fled along the jammed coast road east toward Les Issambres. He was not happy.

"We are lucky we got out alive," he wrote. "You left huge piles of brush along the access road—just perfect to feed the fire! That is completely irresponsible, monsieur!"

I was glad he and his wife were okay, but I didn't appreciate the tone of menace in his email. I resolved to see if we could find other renters for the future. I was planning to burn the brush in the fall.

A few days later, the phones were back up and I spoke with Thierry.

"It was hell," he said. "Everything turned dark at midday from the smoke."

"What did you do?"

"We decided to ride it out rather than risk getting grilled like sardines on the road."

We discussed the house, and he agreed that Monsieur Millot was unhappy. "He is finding fault with everything," Thierry said. "He doesn't like the kitchen. He doesn't like the bathrooms. He doesn't like the fire."

"And especially," I said, "he doesn't like the rent. I'm charging him twice what he used to pay."

"You are very lucky, *Amérloque*! Everybody else burned, except for you!"

It was true. I counted my blessings and praised God for his goodness and his protection. Apparently it was not his plan for us to lose this small piece of his paradise on earth so soon.

My next trip to France was just one month later. I had set up interviews in Paris with top government officials, most of whom I had known for years, to explore the secret nuclear and defense cooperation between the United States and France that had been put in jeopardy by the recent hostility over the Iraq War. After all, enemies didn't betray one another, except by creating false friendships, as Hitler did with Stalin for the purposes of invading Poland. The thesis of my new book was that the depth of the French betrayal of the United States must be measured by the breadth of our two centuries of friendship. From a variety of sources in the United States, I had learned of a secret deal between Presidents Nixon and Pompidou in 1972 whereby the US helped the French develop thermonuclear weapons, so I wanted to present what I had learned to people I suspected had been on the French side of the operation. I also planned to gate-crash the Quai d'Orsay's annual conference of French ambassadors to corner Foreign Minister Dominique Galouzeau de Villepin, one of the villains of my book. I had an invitation from an old friend who was now an ambassador and would be attending the conference.

But before Paris, I wanted to stop by Les Sources for dinner with Alexis to get a better idea of what had happened during the fire. So I flew down to Nice from Stockholm, where we had been vacationing (and I, writing) at Christina's farm.

I drove down the coast road from Fréjus, and once I reached Les Issambres, the scenes were horrifying. The hillsides had been reduced to blackened trunks and stubble. The fire had consumed everything that was green, but because of the speed of the burn it left tree trunks standing, like the ranks of some ancient army stopped in its tracks by the angel of death. The town of Sainte-Maxime was untouched, but the hills beyond it had been torched, exposing huge expanses of white rock I had never seen before.

The rocky access road to Alexis's house climbed the singed hillside laterally, revealing for the first time stone walls and terraces built generations ago but submerged in dense vegetation until now. Alexis was lucky to have a house left. The oak rafters of his outdoor pantry and covered veranda were charred. All around the house, the hillside had burned.

"Wait until you see this," he said, handing me a glass of rosé.

We walked up the stone steps behind the low-roofed house to his heart-shaped pool.

"Look at the chairs! They've melted into the stones!"

It was a curious site. The pool was clean and the filter was running and water was trickling down the rock waterfall he had built at the pointed end of the heart, but on both sides, there were large white gobs of plastic, blackened at the edges, that looked like Dalí's watches.

Here and there you could make out a leg or an arm jutting out of the hardened mess, but that was it.

"How are you ever going to get the plastic off the stone?" I wondered.

"Oh, don't worry. Thierry will take care of it."

Inside, one of the girlfriends I had seen before was making us an omelet with foie gras for dinner.

"Hello, Florence," I said. She was medium height, with dark blonde hair and a spectacular body, dressed in a tight tank top and fashionably torn denim shorts that revealed her curves. I started to ask her what she thought of what had happened.

"Don't worry about her," Alexis said dismissively. "She's just here to cook and to clean and to do the other things a man needs to have done."

The words hit her like the mistral whips the trees. I was embarrassed and couldn't believe Alexis's attitude, nor could I comprehend why Florence just seemed to take it.

But Alexis wasn't done with her. As we started into a fresh bottle of rosé, he grabbed her behind and fondled her. "There are so many young women in Paris like Florence. You offer them the opportunity to come down to the Côte d'Azur, the sun and the sea and the restaurants and the discos, and they just hop on a train. Right, Florence? Don't you enjoy la Côte? Even if you have to put up with an old fart like me?"

"Yes," she said meekly, without turning to face us. But I could see from her neck that she was turning red.

Alexis didn't seem to notice or to care. He was in his early sixties, with thinning white hair, a broad sunburned forehead, large hairy hands, and a developing paunch. He was not good-looking, but he was not ugly, either. I could easily imagine him in a white coat and a dentist's lamp, scooting closer on a rolling chair and saying, "Open wide." Somehow he made it up the kilometer-long rutted dirt road to his house in a low-slung BMW he drove down from Paris. He wanted the girls to know he had plenty of money and was prepared to spend it on them but that he had specific expectations in exchange. He had many redeeming qualities: he was seemingly generous, hospitable, and occasionally witty. And he had introduced me to virtually everyone I had gotten to know in the village. But his way with women I found odious—and inexplicable.

OVER THE NEXT TWO DAYS, before my interviews in Paris, I spent countless hours crashing through the brush with a handheld branch cutter, extending the paths I had cut in the summer. My property had been almost completely spared by the fire, except for a tiny portion of forest at the very top, above the upper spring. The only other casualty was the cistern lock. The firefighters had broken it and nearly drained the cistern to fight the fire. A happier theft of water, I couldn't imagine!

The strangest thing of all was the total silence at night. No cicadas, no birds, no bats flying at sunset—just a deafening silence echoing off the barren, scorched hills. Still, as I sat down to dinner outside, I realized I was falling in love with this house, this hillside, and the valleys below, even with the devastation caused by the fire.

Then on the morning of the thirtieth of August, I was working on my laptop in the upstairs salon when I heard an ominous droning sound. I went out to the solarium and it became more distinct. It sounded almost like the soundtrack of a World War II movie, the drone of heavy propellers in the distance, unseen but approaching, carriers of death and destruction. Suddenly, from behind the mountain that hides our view of Saint-Tropez I saw a lumbering big-bellied plane, and then a second one, and then a third. As they got closer, flying just above the ridgeline across from my house to the south, I realized they were Canadair firefighters, and the roiling clouds just beyond the ridgeline began to make sense. As I looked closer, the white and gray clouds were tinged with columns of orange. Someone had ignited another forest fire, and this one was just across from my house! The ridgeline was just a kilometer away as the crow flies, but twice that distance on foot because of the plummeting hillside and

the valley in between. I had no idea how much time it would take for the fire to reach me, but the mistral was blowing my way.

I rushed downstairs and started doing all the things I had read about in the town fire safety brochure. I ran around the outside of the house closing the shutters, turning off the gas, and putting the rental car in the garage, then ran back inside and filled the bathtub and rolled wet towels to put under the doors. I went upstairs and peered through the closed shutters. More Canadairs were approaching, and now I could see flames above the ridgeline.

Lord God, I prayed, *your plans are so wondrous, so incomprehensible, so all-encompassing. I know you have a plan for me and this place, and you have already shown me once that it does not involve destruction by fire. Lord, let me deserve your graciousness. Spare us once again, Lord. We will work hard to fructify this, your great, good creation. And with your blessing, we will make oil.*

I resolved to dig my way to the olive trees Thierry had told me about, to clear the brush from around them, and to learn to prune them so they would bear fruit again.

An hour later, the clouds blew away, the flames died down, and the Canadairs went home. Praise the Lord!

Boar Hunt

I flew back to Nice after my interviews in Paris in mid-September and worked furiously on my new book over the next month. During the afternoons, I continued to explore the mountain.

At the top of Paradise South, I stumbled upon what appeared to be a terrace, gently sloping across the hill. As I followed it upward, I saw that the edge had been carved by machines out of the rock. It wasn't a terrace; it was a road! I was excited, because on the maps you could see the switchbacks all the way up to the fire road way above, but no one knew where it started or where to find it. The brush had been left to grow for so long it had become a seamless blanket covering rock and spring and ravine alike. And yet, beneath it all along was this road. I bushwhacked my way up for an hour or so, nearly losing it at the switchbacks, until it dead-ended in the ravine.

Straight up, beyond an outcropping of rocks, I could see the fire road, perhaps three hundred meters above me. Here, the whole hillside had burned. The skin of the cork oaks had blackened with char, but the fire had passed so quickly that it burned only the foliage of the brush. You might think that burned brush would be easy to clear, but it's not. In fact, the heather becomes rock-hard when partially burned, and once the trunks become more than two inches thick, they are impossible to break. An odor of death hung over the forest like mist after a rain.

I thought I might cut a path straight up to the rocks and the fire road, and for several days I worked on hands and knees with the branch cutter, clearing twenty meters at a stretch. But once I reached the rocks, it became clear that they were simply impossible: too big and too sheer. There was no way around them without ropes.

So I went back to the road and to the old maps. Sure enough, they showed that the road continued all the way to the top of the mountain. I had merely lost its trace, lured into a futile shortcut.

At dusk, the boar come out from hiding to forage. I could hear them in the dark, wheezing and snorting. Thierry came over one evening with a rifle equipped with a telescopic sight, a Maglite, and a silencer. It was my first boar hunt—and it was totally illegal.

We posted ourselves at the waist-high railing of the pool terrace with a bottle of rosé, overlooking what Thierry was now calling the olive orchard. Directly below us was a semicircle of cleared earth that could have been the foundations of a tower, and then a steep drop into dense brush. We were on a promontory overlooking the valley and the sea. In fact, if marauders wanted to invade this area from the sea, they would have to maneuver directly below us to reach the mountain pass and the hinterland beyond.

"That's why this area is called the Massif des Maures," Thierry said.

"And exactly who were these Maures?"

Both of us knew the answer, but this was part of the sport.

"Why, the Maures were the *bougnouls.* The Arabs," he said.

"They were not just any Arabs. Arabs had never crossed the Mediterranean until the mid-seventh century, after the death of Muhammad," I said. "The Maures were the invading Muslim hordes, the ones who cut off the papyrus trade between Europe and North Africa and brought on the Dark Ages. They are the ones who decimated the coastal cities and drove the trading class inland, where they built fortified castles on the hilltops and became feudal lords. They began in Andalusia, in Spain, and came all the way up into the heartland of France, to Poitiers, destroying everything in their path like locusts. We are standing on the last stronghold of Christendom in this area."

Thierry put a hand to his ear. "Listen," he said.

I heard it, too. A slight rustling in the brush below us.

"How can you see anything?" I said.

"I can't—until their eyes catch the moonlight. Then I turn on the torch and shoot."

He tapped the enormous flashlight taped to his rifle in line with the barrel.

The rustling came closer, and we began to hear low grunts in the brush. I took a sip of rosé from the silver goblet I had brought from the States and marveled at Thierry's rudimentary fire-control system. But then, you couldn't buy night-vision gear in France. In fact, you couldn't even buy a rifle without a license—and anything having to do with government was anathema to Thierry, not for political reasons, but on principle. He was a free man, and they had no right to control him as long as he wasn't endangering others. He had a clear field of fire into the thicket, with no houses in sight until the far side of the valley, a good kilometer away. Why should he not hunt the boar? Especially when they did such damage. But in France, it was completely illegal unless you joined a hunt club and went on organized hunts and paid a lot of taxes and registered your gun. What was the fun of that?

Suddenly, he switched on the light and I saw the beast: it was dark, low, and long, its snout rooting into the ground, completely oblivious to us. It had just thrust its head out from the thicket when Thierry fired once, and we heard a sudden crashing as the beast tried to escape.

"*Ho-la-la!*" he said. "I must have missed. You made too much noise pouring the wine."

"I didn't make any noise pouring the wine," I said. "I was very careful not to make noise pouring the wine."

"It's true. You are not like Albert. Albert came with me and Asterix and Obelix—right here, the same spot. He was sitting on a folding chair. We had three barrels on the railing, and every couple of minutes he would reach into his pocket and swish around, crackling. 'Bastian? Would you like a bonbon?' he'd say, then pull out a piece of candy and take off the plastic wrapper and offer it to Bastian. He never stopped!"

"Did you get the boar?"

"Ha! No way. But now we must go down below and see if we can find it."

We scrambled down to the clearing below the pool. Thierry had unstrapped the Maglite from his rifle and started inspecting the brush that fell off below.

"He must have gone in there," he said, pointing. "Careful! If I just wounded him, he could charge."

The drop-off was steep, and neither of us had gloves, so we clambered down step by step, trying to avoid the spines of Scotch broom and the ground vines, while listening intently for a wounded animal. When we reached the maquis, we couldn't see a thing. The darkness was palpably thick like the walls of a cave. And no sign of a demon-pig.

"I'm sure I hit him," Thierry said. "He can't have gone far."

We pushed into the brush, and to my surprise, it leveled out onto a terrace—a terrace Thierry believed had been planted with olive trees. We fanned out in opposite directions but heard nothing except our own crunching steps at the edge of the deep. After ten minutes or so, we were ready to give up when Thierry shouted.

"Over here!"

The boar had fallen right where we had started, just slightly to one side. In the dark, we hadn't seen the beast, rolled over on its side. Thierry had hit it in the heart, and it just dropped. The crashing noise we had heard initially must have been the rest of the herd running away.

Dead, the boar wasn't as big or as heavy as it had looked alive. We carried it by the legs up to the garage, where Thierry arranged a skinning station, roping the beast by the hind trotters to the rafters.

I brought up a wheelbarrow to catch the blood and the innards and went inside to get another bottle of rosé.

As we were celebrating the kill, Thierry told me more about the olives.

"You've got dozens of trees," he said. "Perhaps more. What luck!" But they were all still buried in the brush. If I wanted them to produce, I had to clear around them and learn to prune them.

"You'd be better clearing the whole terrace, not just around the trees. The more you clear, the easier it becomes."

ALBERT FILLED IN THE MISSING PIECES ABOUT THE FIRE.

He was living alone at this point, having divorced his second or third wife, and had purchased a ruined townhouse in the village for his retirement. I would stop by whenever I was here by myself, and he'd show off his latest project, and we would wind up eating dinner together—usually up at my place, since his was still a mess. He was the same generation as Alexis, around fifteen years my senior, but had spent his professional life around models and journalists, traveling the world as artistic director for *Air France Magazine*. So we would swap war stories and drink late into the night. He was the first person in the area to sport the five-day Italian beard, and being half-Italian with a deeply tanned domed forehead, his graying whiskers made him look dashing, not dirty. His war stories invariably involved the fashion models he escorted to Tahiti and Martinique and Venice and Timbuktu and how in the isolation of the photo shoot they often just couldn't help falling for an older, distinguished man. He and Alexis had shared women at some point, either an ex-wife or a girlfriend. It gave them a familiarity with each other that wasn't always respectful.

"We were all down in the village," Albert said. "Bastian, me, and Marcel, when Alexis phoned from Juan-les-Pins."

"He told me he had gone there with some girl."

"Yeah. He asked us if we would go up and watch his house to keep it from burning."

"And did you?"

"What do you think? I put some hose in my Land Rover and when we reached the house the rafters were still on fire. So we put them out. If we hadn't gone up, he wouldn't have a house left."

"Funny," I said. "He never mentioned that."

"No, he wouldn't," Albert said.

The Artist

Christina came back with me in early October. We were planning on building a stone terrace around the pool, and she wanted to make sure it turned out right. I was comfortable doing tile and electricity and all sorts of odd jobs, but conceiving a geometric structure in space was beyond me. Whenever we had done structural work on our houses, it was always Christina who had the eye.

The problem was that the pool was surrounded by dirt and dead grass, with the tiniest of terraces at one end overlooking the maquis. It was more of a tiny front porch than a terrace, just large enough for two recliners—or three rifles. We intended to spend a lot of time around the pool and wanted at least a six-hundred-square-foot space paved with a yellow Brazilian stone I had found at a local stone gallery. But the whole area was on a slope. How did you lay a terrace on a slant?

"Obviously you don't, my American friend," said Thierry. "That's why man invented machines."

As he walked back and forth over the ground in front of the pool, listening to Christina explain her idea, you could see him digging and shaping in his head.

"You see where the rock comes down over here," he said. "We will follow the contours to make a bench from one end to the other."

"No straight angles," Christina said.

"*Bon dieu*! Of course not!" Thierry exclaimed, pretending offense. "The bench will be exactly the height of ordinary chairs, so you can sit on it and eat at tables if you like."

Neither end of the terrace would be squared off, either, but culminate in elegant curves with a view of the mountains and the vineyards and the sea.

If Thierry had the vision, Asterix was the man with the calculator. He measured the area of the finished terrace and gave us a price per square meter. It was a fair price, and we immediately agreed.

As we waited for them to start the work, Christina and I drove through the fire-ravaged hills and walked areas that had been previously impassible. One of our favorites was called Les Beaucas. Except for a new winery up on the hilltop and two or three houses along the twisting "scenic" road from the village to the highway, it was totally deserted: a vast, mountainous wilderness in all directions, tumbling down to the sea. Because of the fire you could see through the charred tree trunks and brush to the rocks and the paths and the stone terracing walls that had been hidden until then. The fire was Nature's striptease.

When I told Albert about discovering the new winery, he joked. "When you go home for dinner, just don't forget the salt." It was about as far from civilization as you could get in this part of France. The nearest store was probably a good fifteen kilometers away.

Thierry showed up with his truck and a backhoe a few days before we were scheduled to leave, and it was fascinating to watch him work. He manipulated the joystick with a delicacy hard to imagine for so much steel and horsepower. He made the bucket nibble at the dirt until he uncovered the buried water line feeding the pool. At the far side, he nibbled again until he exposed the electric line, and not a mark on either. Then he used a perforating drill to break the rock, scooping the debris into his truck. By the end of the day, he had leveled a six-hundred-square-foot area where they planned to pour a fifteen-centimeter base of reinforced cement for the patio stones. I never once saw him bring out a level, but it was perfectly flat.

When we came back at Christmas with Diana and Simon, the work was done, and we had Christmas lunch in the sun on the new patio. It was stunning and seemed even larger than what we had planned. The pale yellow-and-white stones were a cleaned mirror of the dried grasses of the hillside in summer. Thierry had even rounded the edge of the bench in the rock, using the same tinted cement in which he had set the stones.

"That's what I like about Thierry," Christina said. "You can just talk to him and walk through your idea, and he comes up with something even better."

"He's a real artist, not a pretend artist like Harold," I said. "He sculpts the earth and the rocks and uncovers their hidden beauty."

Increasingly, that was becoming my aspiration with Les Sources. Not to create something out of nothing, as I did as a writer, but to uncover God's secret forms and pleasing symmetries in the exuberant clutter of his creation, pruning to bring order out of apparent chaos.

The End of Something

The midnight New Year's Eve dinner in France is called *le réveil-lon*, meaning something akin to a watch party. Alexis and Albert invited us to the bash they were jointly preparing at the sheep farm. It was going to be an elaborate affair, with oysters and foie gras and a *daube* of wild boar Albert had acquired from a local hunter, an assortment of vegetable dishes including *pommes dauphinoises* done in the oven, and several fruit tarts from the baker who lived next door to Albert in the village. Alexis planned to buy several cases of expensive wines and vintage champagne and asked each couple to contribute 150 euros to the cost. Christina and I thought that was eminently fair, since New Year's Eve dinner at any restaurant would have been that much per person.

But as soon as we arrived at around 10:00 p.m., we could see something was amiss. Alexis and Albert were standing at the flat soapstone sink, shucking oysters, and seemed to be in the midst of an argument. As we said our greetings all around, Albert turned away, trying to mask his anger. Altogether we were a dozen guests. Albert had brought the widow of an old friend, Martine. It was unclear if he was dating her or just taking her out as a kindness so she wouldn't be alone on New Year's Eve.

I handed over the envelope with our 150 euros to Alexis, trying to be discreet. The French generally don't like to talk about money openly. But Alexis was different.

"Ha! You see, Albert? The Americans have no problem paying. They are normal people."

Albert just muttered and leaned into the oyster he was shucking, his hand wrapped in a dishrag. I could tell he didn't want to make a scene.

Alexis poured us champagne and went around the fireplace filling up the crystal flutes of the other guests. When he got to Albert by the sink, whose glass was empty, he poured just two fingers.

"And for the stingy, a stingy pour," he said.

"Stop," Albert muttered, positioning the opened oyster with its fellows on a platter.

A Belgian neighbor we hadn't met before asked me about the war in Iraq.

"I hear you are a writer," he said. "Does the American press celebrate the independence of the French as the Europeans do—not joining Bush in his folly?"

"That depends," I said. "When the Democrats supported the war in the beginning, so did the media. But once the insurgency started and the Democrats broke with Bush, the media started to portray de Villepin—at least, those who knew his name—as someone with remarkable foresight."

"He just saw the obvious," Alexis jumped in. "What anyone but your hero Bush couldn't see."

Normally Alexis hated talking politics, and whenever I saw him in company with Thierry or Albert or Bastian, he would cut me off if one of them asked me a question.

"Politics is so boring," he would say. "Let's talk about something interesting, like Florence." And he would begin to soliloquize in very crude terms on the shape of her body and the type of acts he liked to perform.

Tonight, he had decided to show off. And I became the butt of his remarks, apparently because of my friendship with Albert. What was it between them?

We ate oysters and drank champagne for well over an hour, and there was enough chatter that Christina and I managed to have an actual conversation with our Belgian neighbors, who it turned out were very pro-American, despite his opening provocation.

Just after 11:00 p.m., Florence put a large wooden cutting board on the kitchen counter and Alexis brought out the foie gras from the fridge, wrapped in foil. As he unveiled it—it was an entire duck liver, nearly two hands long, probably weighing close to a kilo—Albert moved to Alexis's side and gently tapped his right hand, the one holding the long, thin knife.

"You should let me do the honors," he said quietly.

"So you are the host now?" Alexis said, turning toward the rest of us but gesturing toward himself.

"I brought the foie gras—and the *sanglier*."

"We've been through that already. And I spent fifteen hundred euros on the champagne and the wines. You see the Château d'Yquem we are about to drink? One hundred seventy-five euros a bottle. And there are three of them to go with the foie gras, all chilled to a perfection, and all opened."

"The champagne was cheap. Less than thirty euros a bottle," Albert said.

"The Pauillac *premier grand cru* we will drink with the *sanglier*, the Chateau Grand-Puy Ducasse, was nearly one hundred euros a bottle. And there are four of those."

I was stunned, and the Belgians and the rest of the guests were embarrassed. It was more appropriate dinner conversation to discuss Florence's body and sexual talents than it was to discuss the price of what we were eating and drinking. In France, it just wasn't done.

"*Allez*, I will serve," said Florence, easing the knife away from Alexis. He sat down with a grunt. Albert found a seat at the far end of the table. Both of them were in a huff.

As the new year approached and we sat down at the formal table to dig into the boar stew, I suggested we say the blessing.

"Alexis? You are the host," I said.

"What for? To a god who doesn't listen? I'm not wasting my breath."

I looked around the table and held out my hands, as we normally do in my house. The other guests looked at each other, shrugged mostly in good humor, and joined hands. I said a brief blessing—not wanting to test the patience of the formally Christian and Jewish French—thanking God for our gathering and for the fine food and wine and for bringing us back to France after so many years. As a year of conflict was coming to an end and something new was about to begin, I asked that God's blessing be with each of us.

"And all God's people say…?" I ended.

Silence. No one seemed to know how prayers ended.

"Amen!" Christina and I said together, and they laughed.

I learned what had happened in bits and pieces over the next couple of days. Alexis was miffed that Albert refused to pay his 150 euros, and Albert was shocked that Alexis even asked him to pay, given that he had brought the foie gras and the wild boar.

From Thierry I learned the crowning idiocy.

Albert had gone to pick up the three raspberry tarts Alexis had ordered from the baker. As she tied the boxes together, she rang them up on her cash register.

"Albert said that Alexis had already paid, he was just picking them up," Thierry said. "But the baker's wife said no, the money was due. Albert insisted, and eventually she must have relented."

"Indeed," I said. "We ate the tarts, that's for sure. They were great."

"But who paid?" Thierry wondered. "The baker's wife says they never got paid—not by Alexis, who said it was up to Albert, and not by Albert."

From that time on, the two became mortal enemies, despite their thirty years of friendship—and all over 150 euros that was probably a wash anyway.

The Truffle Market

A few days later, Christina and Diana drove down to the plain in Grimaud to ride, so I took Albert up on his invitation to visit the weekly truffle market in the village of Aups, around an hour's drive. At the last minute, I called Thierry to see if he was free.

"Aups?" he said. "Why not? I'm sure we will find the secret to Bastian's *sale caractère* in Aups. That's where he's from." The two of them were constantly ribbing each other, but it was good-natured fun.

Simon, now ten, piled into the back of Albert's Land Rover Defender with Thierry.

"So, Simon," he said. "You have lost all your French?"

"A bit," Simon said. "Our teachers in Maryland have terrible accents. And they give me bad grades because I can't spell."

He and Diana were in the French immersion program of the Montgomery County public schools. To my mind, Simon's verbal skills more than compensated for his deficiencies in math and spelling. Even his teacher in France thought so. He could talk rings around the hens in Silver Spring, and I suppose they didn't appreciate it.

"So what did you do for New Year's Eve?" Thierry went on.

Albert swiveled his head and gave Thierry a dirty look.

"Not you, Albert. I know what you did! I was asking Simon."

"Diana and I went to see friends from school in Sainte-Maxime."

"Good! And did you get home before your parents, or did they have to drive dead drunk past all the gendarmes to pick you up?"

"No. We stayed the night."

"Too bad! The gendarmes would have loved to catch an American," Thierry said. "That would be real sport."

We had to park on the outskirts of town because of the market. Like many towns in the Haut Var, Aups was built into a hillside, surrounded by dense woods, with narrow medieval streets near the top. The village square with its fountain and plane trees was surrounded by pastel-shaded facades from the nineteenth and early twentieth centuries, some of them still bearing bullet impacts from the Nazi occupation. Everywhere the truffle sellers had set up makeshift tables shaded by colorful parasols to keep the truffles from drying out.

"They say people from Aups like Bastian are very stingy," Thierry said. "You see how they even cover their truffles with tea towels?"

He was right. Hardly anyone actually displayed their truffles outright, keeping them instead in small wicker baskets covered with red-and-white kitchen towels.

"Why is that?" I asked.

"They go on a diet," Albert said.

"They lose weight drying out," Thierry explained. "And since they are sold by the kilo, the truffle sellers lose money."

How much money could you really lose by exhibiting your truffles in the open air, I wondered.

"Ha!" Thierry said. "Look at the prices and you'll see."

One gnarled old man with a black beret was sitting on a crate, surveying the crowd like a hawk while pretending to pare his fingernails with a pocket knife. He had a single basket on a small table and had written the price in chalk on a slate.

"It's only seventy euros," I said, pointing. "That's not too bad."

"Look closer," Thierry said. "It's seventy euros per one hundred grams. That makes seven hundred euros per kilo."

The oak forests above the village were said to be prime truffle-hunting grounds and were closely guarded to prevent poaching. One year, a thirty-seven-year-old farmer was keeping vigil during the night at the beginning of the season, in November, when he heard someone in the underbrush with a dog. He fired off two cartridges from his shotgun—and killed the man. At his trial, he said he had only been trying to scare him off and got unlucky.

"What does it take to train a truffle dog?" I asked. Churchill's nose was so good that he could smell a rotting deer bone in the forest from hundreds of yards away. Surely I could train him to hunt truffles.

"I keep telling you, American. You don't have the right soil at Les Sources for truffles. You need limestone and a high pH. Your soil is acidic. And besides, Churchill is a goof."

Yellow Labs were goofy, it's true. But Churchill could also behave when he needed to. The first time we took him to a French restaurant, the autumn when we put our kids in the local schools, we drove down to Sète, a seaside resort south of Montpellier. The restaurant was so packed we were back to back with other diners. The four of us sat at a small round table by the port, with Churchill underneath. Churchill was so long that his head stuck out at one end and his tail from the other, but he never budged an inch during the whole meal. Afterward, he got his treats.

"He can be trained," I insisted. "When I brought him through Customs in Paris, I had to take him out of his box on a leash. I said, 'De Gaulle, *assis*!' And he sat."

"De Gaulle or Churchill, I'm telling you. There are no truffles on your hillside."

Albert had wandered off while we were chatting. We caught up to him at a table hidden on a side street.

"Now *those* are truffles," he said, nodding. "All the rest are just Provençal imitations of the Périgord black."

A small man with dark hair and a plastic cup of red wine was seated behind the table next to a peasant woman with sun-darkened skin and heavy wrinkles. Albert asked them in Italian the price of their truffles.

"Fifteen hundred euros, *signore*," the man said.

"You see? These are Italian truffles. White truffles. The best," he said. "They come from Alba, which is near my hometown."

"Velli?" I said. "There is a town named Velli?" That was his last name.

"Of course!" Albert said. Then he laughed. "It's short for Machiavelli. My brother discovered it by accident driving through the Piedmont a couple of years ago, so he bought a cottage there. We'd never heard of it before."

I didn't yet know any recipes for truffles excerpt for mixing them into an omelet, so I wasn't buying. Albert said he only wanted the Italian white, and they were too expensive here. But after an hour of wandering from table to table, Thierry eventually selected a black truffle the size of a golf ball, weighing just under a hundred grams. It cost him fifty euros.

"We will make many *bocaux* of wild boar pâté with this truffle," he said, holding it up to the light. "And, of course, an omelet for six with an ostrich egg."

"Ostrich egg?" I said.

"From the ostrich farm on the road to Le Muy."

I had a vague recollection of seeing a sign for ostrich meat along the road but had never taken it seriously.

Of course, we stayed for lunch, and each of us had a truffle omelet and some of the hearty red wine from nearby Lorgues. I cut Simon's wine with water, but it made him happily drunk anyway.

As we were eating a fruit tart for dessert, Thierry began to quiz him again on his French.

"So, Simon. You learned while you were at school what the people from Sainte-Maxime are called, right?"

"Yes," he said. "*Les Maximois.*"

"And don't forget *les Maximoises,*" Albert added.

"And Le Plan-de-la-Tour. What are its inhabitants called?" Thierry went on.

That was much harder. I wasn't sure that Simon had learned it, but he surprised me. In France, each town had a special name for its people, as if it were a province or a country. And there are 34,836 of them!

"*Les Plantouriens,*" he said. "And the women are *Plantouriennes.*"

"Bravo! Now for the hardest," Thierry said. "What about the people from Aups? Like our friend Bastian?"

Simon thought for a moment. Then he raised a finger with a huge grin.

"*Les Aupsédés!*" he said.

We cracked up, pounding the table with our hands, for the word was pronounced *obsédé,* which in French meant pervert.

"*Mon dieu,* now there are two of them!" Thierry gasped between laughter. "What are we going to do?"

I was known for making puns in French, pretending I couldn't find the right word, then substituting something that sounded similar but was outrageous. And now Simon was doing the same.

"I will have to tell Bastian that Simon discovered he is an *Aupsédé....* That's him to a T."

We Are Rich

People from the north often idealize the Mediterranean, just like the Paris weather forecasters, as the land of no winter, blue skies, and unlimited sun. But as we learned the previous year, autumn brought cool nights and drenching rains that lasted until the end of November, and winter soon followed with near freezing temperatures at night and, if you were lucky, crisp, clear days when the sun was so bright it could burn you in minutes. But other days were not so lucky, with dense clouds filling the valleys and turning them into white lakes and a damp chill that penetrated you through and through, made worse by the lack of central heating. The convectors Ofilio had installed during the "all-electric" phase that swept France in the late 1970s and early 1980s consumed enormous amounts of energy and did very little to actually heat the house. And the fireplace upstairs where I worked smoked when the mistral blew, just when you needed it the most.

When I came back in mid-April, I learned about the Provençal spring. It was an explosion of primary colors. Bright red poppies burst from the grasses along the roads, along with goldenrod and wild lavender and Queen Anne's lace and a whole assortment of purple, yellow, and blue flowers I had never seen before. (I later learned that the purple ones were a kind of wild orchid called *orchis peint* that stood high on stalks with hanging flowers a bit like snapdragons. The ordinary nettle also had purple flowers, while the *liseron* vines were a bright blue.) April was the season when the Scotch broom became a boon, not a spur, pouring buckets of brilliant yellow across the hillsides. Clouds of white pollen from the heather wrapped around you like cobwebs if you brushed against them.

But most extraordinary were the hillsides that had burned above us. They were now covered with a moss-green carpet and lozenges of yellow and red and purple wildflowers. Here and there leaves sprouted from a charred cork oak. Just six month after the fire had seemingly killed everything, Nature's rebirth had begun.

Spring was also the season of heavy, drenching rains that would sweep across the sky like the magic lantern projection of an El Greco painting. The roiling bright clouds moved quickly, often bringing sheets of rain for ten minutes or a half hour, and then it would clear up and the sun would come out until the next squall. The frequency of these warm rains not only brought the flowers; it created powerful waterfalls that carved hidden channels in the rocks. The Bay of Pigs was overflowing onto the road. When I walk these hillsides and hear the rushing of waters and see the explosion of colors, I think: *What great abundance has our Lord, what inventiveness and glorious variety. He is indeed the Creator of all good things, and I am blessed to have returned from the valley of death to praise his name.*

DURING A BREAK IN THE RAIN, I took dry mortar and boards and a mixing tub up to the cistern and re-cemented the broken hinge of the cover. I sanded down the rusted lid and coated it in oil. I had been putting chlorine tablets in the water so it no longer smelled foul, but there was still a dead mouse floating in the water that I scooped out with the pool skimmer. I found three possible entry points for the mice—a cement aeration tube, the overflow hole, and gaps around the lid—and plugged or screened them all. With the lid open I could hear a strong trickle of water that had to be coming from our springs, which I had reconnected. I had turned off the pump in the autumn, and yet water was pouring from the overflow pipe onto the hillside below. Contrary to what Ofilio had claimed, our cup was running over. We had plenty of water.

But where was the second spring? I took a pick, a shovel, and a trowel up to where the pipes were sticking out of the ground, about four hundred meters straight up from the cistern, and started to dig. I soon discovered we had two main types of rock: sedimentary, which Alexis called *patate*—potato stone, because it split easily into smaller pieces—and white marble. When you hit marble, there was nothing to do except dig around it and hope to excavate the entire stone. It took me an hour to dig two feet down, following the pipe until it disappeared into the marble. There had to be a better way.

One possibility, of course, was that the pipe just continued to plunge deeper into the earth to a capture basin buried below. If so, I wasn't going to uncover it with hand tools. But what if the basin had been carved out of the hillside? Thierry had noticed a suspicious rock formation a few meters beyond where I was digging. The rocks formed a natural niche in the hillside that was overgrown with vines. When I cleared them away, sure enough, the rock face was sweating water.

Perhaps the basin was below. But there was no sign of anything man-made, just vines and dirt and flat, flinty stones flecked with fool's gold. I selected a spot in the middle and began to dig anyway. Here, the earth was different. While not soft or moist, it had more of a gravel consistency, as if it had been washed down the hillside in the rains and collected here. I dug down fifteen centimeters, twenty, and the gravel still came away easily. I cleared a rectangular hole the size of a laptop using the trowel, and then I heard it. The trowel banged against something metallic! When I cleared away more dirt and banged it again, it rang hollow. I felt like a child in a fairy tale. I had discovered the entrance to the buried treasure hall. But instead of a chest full of jewels and gold coins, it was water.

It took me another two hours to clear the gravel, but eventually I uncovered two large iron plates, each with handles welded at either end. When I finally managed to move one of them to the side, I could smell the damp and hear bits of gravel splash into the dark pool below.

Not wanting to foul the spring, I covered it back up and returned the next day with more tools and cleared the whole area. When I finally got both metal plates off, I had to marvel again at the genius of the Swede who had designed the hydraulic system. Despite twenty years of neglect by Ofilio, the water in the catch basin was still clear and deep and pure. I disconnected the aboveground pipe  and climbed down in bare feet into astonishingly cold water until I found the other end, which was clogged with vegetation. When I pulled out the long roots, the suction began immediately and water began gushing out the pipe below.

The bottom was full of mud and small stones, so I stirred it up to get as much of it to drain as possible; then I used a dustpan to scoop out the muck that remained, washing it down with clear water I had set aside in two buckets. As much as I scooped, I could never get the bottom dry because water kept seeping into the basin from the stone. But I got it clean and reset the suction pipe and then the metal covers, knowing it would start flowing again in a matter of hours.

We were rich!

Land of the Lotus Eaters

Thierry came over one evening for drinks so I could show him photographs from my recent trip to Libya, where I had been able to visit the ancient Roman metropolis of Leptis Magna, two hours east of Tripoli along the coast. It was the best-preserved Roman site in the entire Mediterranean outside of Rome itself. Its long paved streets and amphitheater fronting the sea were magnificent. The Romans had even built domed saunas down on the beach that looked like igloos half-buried in the sand.[4]

What interested Thierry most were the pictures I had taken during a drive back from Sirte to Tripoli through the hinterland. The rolling hills south of Misrata were covered with olive orchards as far as the eye could see. But with the torrential spring rains, the valleys had become a vast lake of muddy reddish-brown water, broken only by the tree trunks and the wind.

"That's not how you would imagine Libya," he said.

"Not at all."

Thierry dreamed of taking his Toyota Land Cruiser on safari through the southern Libyan desert along the border with Chad. Just this winter he and Chantal had taken off three weeks and toured a portion of the Moroccan Sahara. The year before, they traveled through southern Algeria. He was attracted to the solitude of the desert. Even

---

[4] See *The Iran House*, chapter 22: "The Stiff."

though they organized these trips with a group of friends—all of them driving specially equipped Toyotas—the vastness of the desert and the knowledge that a single mistake or a breakdown could put all their lives at risk intensified the pleasure. He had rigged his truck with extra tanks for diesel fuel and water and had even fitted it with an outdoor shower. But break an axle on the rocks, or flip over playing on the dunes, and real trouble began.

"I've had it with la Côte," he said. "It's hard to be an honest man and still work here. Look at all the stonemasons you see driving their Porsche Cayennes. If you ever see a guy coming to your house to give you an estimate driving a Porsche Cayenne, you know he's going to charge you double what the work should cost."

"*Encore une voiture de coiffeuse,*" I said. This was our joke about Alexis's BMW. It rode so low to the ground only a hairdresser would dream of driving it on the rocky roads.

"No!" he said emphatically. "The Porsche Cayenne is not *une voiture de coiffeuse. C'est une voiture de voleur*—a thief's car."

He and Chantal were making good money with his construction business, but they were thinking of giving it all up—just as they had in their youth when they rented a farm in the Ardèche and raised sheep. His new dream was to return to the Ardèche and open a hostelry in the middle of the Massif Central, the deserted mountain range in the very center of rural France. He wanted to buy a ruined château or a farmhouse and renovate it himself, and open a restaurant and hotel.

"We will serve extravagant fare, wild game, our own pâté and foie gras and country wines—good, honest food. And we will charge exorbitant prices to the tourists who want to taste the wilderness right here in France."

It was an honest ambition, but I didn't want to encourage him since I enjoyed his company and didn't want them to leave.

"Nobody ever goes to the Ardèche," I said. "There are no tourists there."

"We will make them come."

"How's that?"

"We will become so famous because of Chantal's cooking and our spectacular views that everyone will want to come."

"Hmm," I said. "'Magnificent château with fantastic food in the middle of nowhere. Come, and we will charge you a fortune.' Somehow I don't think that's a catchy idea."

"Mais non," he said. "It is not the middle of nowhere. It's the far end of nowhere. The very dark edge of nowhere. But that's why people will come. To get as far away from Paris and Lyon and Marseille and the Côte d'Azur as they can."

"Dream weekend in Ardèche," I said, mimicking the tourist brochure again. "Fresh snow every night. Thirty below zero. Bring your ski clothes—just not the skis."

"Maybe cross-country skiing," he said sheepishly.

"In all the years you lived in Ardèche raising sheep, how many times did you cross-country ski?"

"Not once," he admitted. "It was too cold."

"Even if you are successful, you will still have to pay all the employment taxes."

"Ah, merde," he said.

That was the last straw. Business owners had to pay employment taxes for each worker that were now running 52 percent on top of their take-home salary. It was very difficult to start a business, and very difficult to end one, even in bankruptcy, because you became liable for labor penalties that could be as much as two years' salary per worker.

"This is why so many people work on the black," he said. "They buy their Porsche Cayennes with cash!"

France had become the land of the lotus-eaters, where few people had any real ambition other than to party, go on vacation, play sports, or go to the summer art and music festivals. There was no point in working hard because you wouldn't be able to get ahead unless you cheated and managed to hide your earnings from the tax authorities. You could see this everywhere in France. The French became completely different people as soon as they got off work. That was when

real life began, whatever it was. They lived for pleasure. And work, by definition, could not be part of this.

It wasn't as if Americans didn't enjoy their leisure or the arts or their pleasures. But there was something very distinct about the French attitude toward work and pleasure. To the French, work increasingly had become the means to pleasure, which they suffered through grudgingly, whereas for most Americans work was what gave you value in life, while pleasure was the reward you enjoyed afterward.

Thierry and Chantal were caught between the two worlds. They wanted to create something with their skills and hard labor. But they didn't want to become slaves to work—especially when government stole the fruit of their labor.

"Let me dream, at least," he said.

"It's more than a dream. You will achieve it—whatever *it* is. But it may be different from what you think. It's the balance that's important," I said. "God wants you to be happy wherever you are, and he has a plan for you."

"So where do I find this plan?" he said with a laugh, filling our empty glasses with rosé.

"It's probably right in front of your nose," I said.

"I see, but I do not see," he said in heavily accented English. "But maybe that is because I have a very big nose."

Finding the Pony

I was on the road a lot that year. After Libya, I started working as a consultant to a consortium of law firms investigating the September 11 attacks. They had expected the US government to uncover documents after the invasion of Iraq that would unmistakably prove Saddam Hussein's involvement in 9/11, as they believed President Bush had claimed, and were nonplussed when that never happened. I had published several articles about Iran's involvement in the attacks, which I had learned from defectors from Iranian intelligence organizations. The lawyers commissioned me to help track down those defectors, depose them, and corroborate their testimony. That first year, the work took us many times to Paris, and to Karlsruhe and Athens, so I based myself at Les Sources instead of crossing the Atlantic repeatedly. Since my next book was on Iran, it was a perfect arrangement, and Les Sources was the perfect place to write.

Our bedroom faced the rising sun. Christina liked to close the shutters so we could sleep later, but in June, while I waited for her to join me with the children, I would wake up early and walk down to the pool and luxuriate in the sudden astonishing heat as the sun broke the crest of the hill and hit my skin like a laser. Every morning, I would stretch out my arms and utter a prayer of thanks. This was God's paradise on earth, there could be no doubt. And what had I done to deserve it? Absolutely nothing. It was a gift, freely given.

Before writing in the morning, I read the Bible. Sometimes I followed the liturgical calendar, but most often I chose a Gospel to read over my stay and punctuated it with psalms I would read aloud to the hills. These were happy times.

In the late afternoons, I started clearing brush from the terrace below the pool. After the stress of travel and dealing with the lawyers, physical labor was revitalizing and cleared my mind. I swapped out the grinder for an ordinary saw blade and cut the tall heather and broom just above the stones, piling it in enormous stacks to burn in the autumn.

Albert joined me one day when I was taking a break. My jeans were drenched, as was my shirt.

"Look! You've got olives!" he said, pointing to the tree I had just uncovered.

I had cut a two-meter swath around the tree, which otherwise had been lost in the wilderness. Albert drew down the fronds to examine them.

"This is a *tanche*," he said. It was the most common species of olive in our region. The fruit was slightly oblong and looked like it would grow to the size of green table olives. "You must have more," he said.

It was hard to see because the brush was so thick. To me, it looked like an impenetrable forest, broken only by the boar runs tunneled close to the ground.

"We need to look from above," he said.

We climbed to the semicircle below the pool that I suspected covered the ruins of an ancient tower. It stood around five meters above the terrace where I had uncovered the olive tree.

"Not high enough," Albert said. "We're still in the brush."

So we went up to the shooting terrace by the pool, a couple of meters higher.

"Ken, you wouldn't have something to drink?" Albert asked. It was around 7:00 p.m., and while the sun was still strong, it had moved to the far side of the house, so we were in the shade.

"What would you like?"

"Perhaps some rosé?"

"I thought you and Alexis considered rosé not to be wine?"

"Don't talk to me about Alexis," he huffed.

I went up to the kitchen and drank nearly a liter of cold water to replenish what I had lost cutting brush, then brought down a bottle of chilled rosé and two silver goblets. We leaned against the railing and drank appreciatively.

"Look at the color of the foliage," Albert said. "If you look closely, you will see that the brush is broken by patches of almost silvery gray. Those are all olives."

"No way!" I said. As I looked, I could see lots of patches of silvery-gray leaves. In fact, the entire terrace was studded with them. But none of them stood higher than the surrounding brush. From here, they just blended into the carpet of foliage.

I knew that Albert had helped Alexis for several years with his olive orchard and had soaked up much of his knowledge. Unlike Alexis, he freely offered what he knew rather than test my ignorance. Alexis had never pointed out the olives on my property, although he had been here several times.

"Why don't you show me," I said.

We set down our empty goblets and donned gloves. Albert pushed into the dense foliage beyond the area I had just cleared.

"They are much closer than you think," he said, holding out a branch so it didn't snap into my face. "Look!"

It was slow going in the wilderness. The bushes were the size of trees and sometimes grew so close together you couldn't squeeze through but had to find a way around. And then there were the prickers. You also had to watch the ground, because in places it dropped off suddenly just as it did up on the hillside. We hadn't pushed more than ten meters in when we found the next olive tree. The trunk was perhaps six inches across, but it had been completely choked by the brush.

"Look at how smooth the skin is!" he said.

He used the word for skin, not bark, and I could see why: there were no scales on this tree, just a silvery smooth skin.

"This one is a *picholine*," he said. "See how the fruit is long and oblong?"

There were fewer olives on this tree, but still, it had fruit. I cut a few of the smaller bushes that surrounded it so I could find it again, and then Albert crashed into the wilderness beyond.

The next tree had five trunks and grew like a bush. "This sometimes happens with regrowths after a fire or a big freeze. Everything froze in this valley in 1956."

"That was nearly fifty years ago," I said. "This is all they have grown in fifty years?"

"Could be, if no one has taken care of them. But it could also be the fire of '92."

He pushed farther along the terrace finding tree after tree, which I marked as best I could. Altogether, we found over a dozen trees. Some of them had grown back from stumps. A few had survived the freeze of '56 and had trunks that must have been nearly ten inches in diameter.

"It's going to take forever to clear all of this," I said.

"*Ouf*," he said. "If you like, I can come up and help you."

So, over the next two days, we cleared the terrace in the evenings, mostly by hand, creating huge piles of brush. The terrace extended for well over a hundred meters, and we found thirty-two trees. As we got to the far end, the ground sloped down instead of dropping off, and there at the bottom was yet another tree!

"This olive grove used to sit on *two* terraces," Albert said. "We've just done the half of it!"

That explained the drop-off. Three meters vertical separated the two terraces, except at the end, where they joined in a sliding turn that a tractor could negotiate. Both terraces had been carved from the hillside long ago with machines.

Albert was a good sport and helped me clear the lower terrace, too, where we found an additional twenty-three trees. Nearly half of them had olives, despite not having been pruned in decades.

"Ken, you are rich! You have more trees than Alexis."

"I thought you didn't want to talk about Alexis?"

"It's true," he laughed. "Except when he is an ass. And he is always boasting about his olives."

"That is true."

Just like the water up on the hillside, I was sitting on hidden wealth I had never suspected—nor, apparently, had the previous owners. But to find it I had to look, and then recognize what I was seeing, and then clear away the clutter. Without that, it was just chaos.

So bringing order out of chaos was often just a question of stripping away everything that was unnecessary to find the underlying form.

Or as Ronald Reagan liked to put it, when you found a barn full of manure, there had to be a pony in there somewhere.

With Albert's help, I found the pony.

First Harvest

That autumn I was on the road again with the lawyers. I managed a short trip to Les Sources in mid-September to check on the olives, which were maturing well. Then it was more travel until early November, when I had planned three weeks of writing time at Les Sources. Albert made dinner for me the night I arrived at his place in the village, a huge fire of cork oak sparking and popping behind the bead curtain of his fireplace.

"You can take all the wood you want from my place," I said.

"That's what I have been doing," he said sheepishly.

"I can see that!" I laughed. "That's good!"

I had tons of wood and wanted to encourage him. The more Albert took, the less I would have to burn on the hillside.

"And so how goes it with the American?" he asked.

"Life is good. God is great."

"And?" he said with a sly smile. It was a repartee I had developed while living at Les Sources. Albert knew it by heart but loved to hear me repeat it, probably because it was so un-French and so politically incorrect.

"And Jesus is not a Muslim," I said, and he laughed.

After he poured me a glass of rosé he became serious. "You say that all the time, and we always laugh. But why?"

"Well, life is good, is it not?"

"That's true," he agreed.

"And look around you at God's creation. God is great, is he not?"

"If you say so," he said. "I suppose there's no one else who could have created all that. But Jesus?"

"Muslims are convinced that Jesus is a Muslim and have adopted him as a prophet. But it's not the same Jesus that we worship as Christians."

"How is that?"

"Muhammad refers to Jesus many times in the Quran and calls him a prophet. But he specifically denies that he is the son of God. 'God did not have a son.' Then, like a good lawyer, whoever wrote the Quran makes the subsidiary argument: if Jesus *was* the son of God, then he could not have died on the cross, because God would never have allowed his son to be crucified."

"I guess you can't have it both ways," Albert said. "What do you think of this rosé?"

"It is particularly fruity," I said, and sipped again. "Crisp red fruits. Red currants. Where did you get it?"

He was pouring the wine from a pitcher, not a bottle.

"I discovered this small vineyard in La Motte." That was a village just beyond the autoroute, about a thirty-minute drive. "It's called Canta Rainette."

"Does that mean something, Canta Rainette?"

"In Provençal, it means *ze zinging frog*," he said in English.

"I can see why the frog sings. It is delicious."

"Plus, it's only two euros a liter."

"Even better!"

When I first met Albert, his house had been stripped to the beams and the cement floor. Bastian was working in the second living room beyond the courtyard with an enormous hose spraying plaster onto the walls. Now, more than a year later, he was nearly finished with the renovations. In the second living room, he had hung from the ceiling a magnificent cedar-strip canoe he had brought back from Alaska during one of his photo shoots, shiny with varnish over the wooden ribbing and inlay. In the living-dining room by the kitchen, he had installed three-foot-long crocodile sculptures he had carved from eucalyptus trunks. The kitchen was set off by a basalt bar counter, where we were drinking. Albert was glazing onion rings in a mixture of butter and olive oil in a skillet. When they were done, he added two slices of calf's liver and opened a bottle of Beaumes-de-Venise. Most people thought Beaumes-de-Venise was a sweet muscat, but we were drinking the red, and it was rich and smooth.

"Didn't you used to live in Beaumes-de-Venise?" I said.

"Never!"

"Where was it, then?"

"Les Baux."

"Les Baux-de-Provence? No way!"

Christina and I had visited the tiny village above Marseille two years ago when I was finishing *The French Betrayal of America*. We found the owner of the famous restaurant, L'Oustau de Baumanière, where Jacques Chirac had hosted Saddam Hussein for lunch during their initial courtship years ago. When my book came out, critics said that I had made up the whole sequence because Saddam was known to favor expensive French and Italian tailors who would never have dressed him like a teenager. What they didn't know was that the restaurant owner, now over eighty, had retrieved his photo albums and shown me the menu and pictures of Saddam and Chirac at a table ,and later at the bullfight with the village boys. In all of them, Saddam was wearing a gaudy seersucker suit, just as I described in the book.[5]

"It's the size of a postage stamp, up on the rock," I said, referring to the village. The likelihood of us both having a connection to Les Baux was infinitesimal.

"Wait. How do you call the people of Les Baux?" I asked.

Albert scratched his head. "*Les Bausasciens? Les Baumanesques?*" He took a slow sip of wine until it dawned on him. "No, wait. *Les Baussencs.* And the women are *les Baussenques.*"

---

[5] Kenneth R. Timmerman, *The French Betrayal of America* (Three Rivers Press, 2004), 40.

I was impressed. Albert explained that he had bought a farm-house on the outskirts of town that he planned to renovate after he retired from Air France—until he got sidetracked.

"Marie-France," he said, longingly.

"Marie-France?"

"She was the wife of the *raseur* who owned olive orchards outside of Les Baux. He made a killing on those orchards. They had a special *appellation contrôlée* and sold the oil for a fortune. He was a crook."

As I pulled the story out of him, Albert and Marie-France became lovers. He would time his visits to his unrenovated farmhouse to out-of-town business trips by her husband.

"We always stayed in the château," Albert said. "I made love to her in her marriage bed while he was gone. It drove her wild."

One day, of course, the husband returned early and Marie-France panicked. She roused Albert from sleep and hustled him down a back staircase to the olive press.

"He never suspected a thing," Albert said. "And I swear to God, I had nothing to do with his arrest."

"Arrest?"

"The tax authorities came after him for trafficking oil. He was mixing cheap Algerian olive oil with oil from Les Baux and selling it for the same price. I suppose that's how he made his fortune. But now he's in jail and his bank accounts have been confiscated."

"So why didn't you stay with Marie-France?" I asked.

"Ouf—you know."

The shrug of his shoulders suggested all kinds of answers. Perhaps he and Marie-France found they were incompatible. Perhaps, with the husband in jail, the thrill was gone. Perhaps she found a younger man with money. Whatever it was, he didn't want to discuss it.

"Did you hear what happened to Florence?" he said to change the subject.

Florence was the hardheaded blonde from New Year's Eve whom Alexis so publicly abused. I knew that she had left him, but not how.

"She showed up on my doorstep in tears in late August," Albert said. "She'd walked all the way down from Alexis's house with her roller bag. In high heels."

It was a two-kilometer trek down to the main road, and parts of the access road were wicked steep. It's a wonder she didn't fall in the ditch.

"And Alexis never offered to give her a ride?"

"Are you joking? That's how he is. I took her to Maxime so she could get a taxi to the airport."

The image of Florence in her high heels and tiny shorts and tank top, her head thrown high and her copper-blonde hair flying behind her as she dragged her roller bag over the rocks and ruts of that dirt road, was too much. I could imagine Alexis sitting on his front porch, laughing as she struggled with her bag, wondering when she was going to give up and turn back and beg for help. And she never did. By the time she reached Albert's house, she had worked herself into a fury. The tears she greeted him with were tears of anger. It was a fitting end to all the abuse Alexis had shown her.

THE NEXT DAY, WE DROVE TOGETHER in his Land Rover up to Callas, about an hour away, a village known for its olive oil (and where the men were *Callassiens*, and the women *Callassiennes*—proving the point that you pronounced all the letters of the village name). This is where Alexis always took his olives to be pressed, often with Albert accompanying him. I needed to buy the regulation twenty-five-kilogram-capacity red olive crates, which were the only containers the mill would accept. They could be stacked five or six high and had aeration holes to prevent the fruit from rotting. I also needed olive rakes and an olive net. While we were there, I purchased a couple of books that explained pruning and grafting techniques, fertilizer, pests, illnesses, and water. They also had a pollination chart showing which varieties were needed to fecundate others.

"How in the world can you tell them apart?" I asked the man in the shop.

"You need a professional," he said, immediately deducing that I was not—at least when it came to olives.

We loaded my new gear into the back of Albert's Land Rover and headed higher into the mountains on switchback roads for lunch in a tiny village called Bargemon. It was perched on a cliff overlooking a deep valley, a bit like Thierry's dream château in the Ardèche. We found a table on the sunny terrace of the village hotel and ate *confit de canard parmentier*, a hearty dish I thoroughly recommend if you can work it off, and drank a thick, tannic Château les Crostes.

"It's mostly hooey," Albert said as we discussed the complexities of pollination. "What you really need is to spray the trees with boron when they begin to flower. That's the key."

"What does that do?"

"Beats me," he laughed. "But it works."

Two weeks later, we began the harvest. I was tremendously excited. It had been raining, and so we watched the weather. Though we could harvest in the rain, it would be cold and less fun. But most important was to get the olives in before the mistral blew. A strong mistral could knock a good portion of the harvest to the ground prematurely.

I spent several summers in Corsica before I married Christina and recalled that the commercial olive groves used tractors to harvest the olives with an attachment that shook the trees. That was not the technique we planned to use—and not just because we didn't have the machines. Machine-harvesting worked best when the olives were fully ripe and ready to fall on their own, in mid to late December. And while harvesting late increased the yield (more on that later), it also decreased the acidity of the oil, making it less fruity, yellow, and more oily. We planned to harvest when a majority of the olives were "turning." But in reality, we had everything from fully ripe *cailletiers* that squished like ripe blueberries when you raked them to completely green *picholine*. In between were those varieties that had turned violet but not yet fully black—*tanche, aglandau, cayon*—and the round *bouteillan*, which could get as large and dark as plums.

All of this I learned as Albert helped me to spread the forty-foot net, with one radius cut to fit around the trunk, from tree to tree. I was shocked to see how brusquely Albert would seize the fronds full of olives and rip the plastic rake through them, taking off leaves and even smaller branches.

"Aren't you worried about damaging the trees?" I said.

Albert just laughed and raked harder. "They are like a French woman," he said. "As long as you take care of them, they are happy. What they don't like is to be neglected."

The same was true, I suppose, of the ground beneath the trees. While I had cut the brush in the summer, I had not been able to clear the stumps, and they caught all the time on the net, sometimes ripping it. Also problematic were the vines. When nothing else grew in Provence, vines could sprout from rocks. They were the worst of all, catching not only the net but your hands.

It was happy work, and we talked as we harvested and stopped often to drink wine. By the end of the day, we had combed the branches of a dozen trees—all the ones that bore olives that year—and put the fruit in crates for the mill.

"They will not do a press run for you with less than two hundred kilos," Albert said once we had loaded the crates into his Land Rover.

"So how do I know it's my oil?" I wondered.

"You don't. They mix it all together. But just wait until next year after you prune the trees. Then you will have your own oil."

I was disappointed when they weighed our crates in Callas. The total harvest came to just 22 kilos. A few days later we returned to pay for the pressing and retrieve the oil—a single plastic jug holding three liters. For that first harvest, it took 7.3 kilos of olives to make just one liter of oil. And that, I learned, was a decent yield. Sometimes it could take as much as 10 kilos per liter. I tried to put on a good face.

"So, for nine euros I spent on the pressing, we got three liters of olive oil. That's just three euros per liter," I said.

Albert laughed. "Plus forty euros for the net, and fifteen euros for the rakes, and another twenty euros for the crates—and twelve hundred euros for your plane ticket."

"Three plane tickets, actually. When you add all the time we've spent, it's a thousand euros per liter!"

"But next year it will be *your* oil," Albert said.

Le Jour du Merci Donnant

After the harvest, we had a week of Indian summer before Thanksgiving. The days were bright and sunny and got up to twenty-two degrees Celsius with no wind. I rented a chain saw and cut down dead trees all over the property—mimosa and eucalyptus that died in last summer's drought and cork oaks that had never recovered from the fire of 1992. I was so hot by lunchtime that I stripped off my wet clothes and jumped into the pool—even though the water temperature was just twelve degrees (fifty-four Fahrenheit).

Water that cold shocks your system. If you try to wade in, you won't. So you either jump in or you don't swim. But once you get out, the cold drops off your skin like a wet shirt. It was warm enough in the sun to have lunch outside in shorts and no shirt.

Thursday was Thanksgiving, and while I missed being with family and friends in the States, I knew I was in for a special treat. Albert had acquired a leg of boar, and Chantal had agreed to cook it for us.

Chantal was the female version of Thierry. Perhaps that's why their marriage had lasted through thick and thin. They got married at twenty, and after two snowy winters and two children with no running water in the Ardèche, they were ready to return to civilization. She ran the business side of their small company and managed the food. That might sound odd to American readers, but Thierry and Chantal were not just into food: they were *really* into food— the type of rich, varied country fare that was gradually going out of existence as more French families fled the countryside and craved for supermarkets. They made their own *saucisson* and pâtés, and bought fatted duck livers to make foie gras, and duck breasts to make *magret*. They regularly purchased sides of pork and lamb from friends in the Ardèche and vegetables and cheeses from local farmers. Eating with them was always a treat.

They lived in a mill house over the river at the end of the village. The houses were all attached, and the cobblestone street was so narrow everyone left their cars in a municipal lot in a nearby field. Their front door looked like the back door of a barn, and you had to step down a steep flight of stone steps to get into the house itself. The big room that served as living room, dining room, and kitchen had the feel of an underground cellar, with thick stone columns and an arched ceiling and the round stone basin of an olive press set in a niche. At the far end, a trapdoor gave onto the river below. Because of the way the land fell off, they had a small balcony overlooking the street and the river. Sylvain and Caroline were now in high school and lived in rooms up above.

I uncorked a bottle of bubbly and served us all around.

"Today is Thanksgiving," I said. "*Le Jour du Merci Donnant.*"

Merci donnant—a literal translation of Thanksgiving invented by professional wag Art Buchwald—had no meaning in French. But every year on the day before Thanksgiving, the *International Herald Tribune* ran Buchwald's original column, where he explained Thanksgiving to the French. Miles Standish became *Kilomètres Deboutish*, the Pilgrims became *Pèlerins*, and Plymouth was now "a famous *voiture américaine.*" The Indians were *Peaux Rouge*, a wink to his hometown football team, the Redskins. As Buchwald explained it, *le Jour du Merci Donnant* began when the *Pèlerins* had raised more corn "than the *Peaux rouges* had killed *Pèlerins.*"

No such holiday existed in France, which gave up thanking God for anything after mean-spirited revolutionaries chopped the head off Marie Antoinette for offering cake to the peasantry. Even the concept was a bit difficult for most Frenchmen to grasp.

"So this is why you say *la grâce*," Thierry said.

The French word for grace is *bénédiction*, or more simply, *prière*, and Thierry of course knew this. *La grâce* is what you offered a bull or a turkey when you agreed not to slaughter them.

We began in high spirits and quickly moved from bubbly to a Château Peyrassol, a red produced on the grounds of a *commanderie* that once belonged to the Knights Templar, a farm compound for pilgrims and fighters on the way to Jerusalem. It was typical of the enormous progress winemakers had made in Provence since the 1980s when the reds were undrinkable. Slightly tannic but with less body and finesse than most Bordeaux, it smelled of the maquis: thyme and rosemary and heather and lavender with just a hint of cistus. Albert and I had stumbled on the vineyard during one of our drives through the countryside, attracted by the bright Templar crosses on the signpost and the ancient stones of the Templar hostel. It went perfectly with the *saucisson* and *rillettes de sanglier* accompanied by glazed onions that Chantal had made.

"So! What about this oil?" Thierry said. "This American olive oil."

"It is not American olive oil," I said. "It came from the hillside *chez Angélus.*"

"But it is made by an American."

"And a Frenchman, if you don't mind," said Albert deliberately. If he had been the type of person to sport a mustache, he would have twirled it as he said this.

"And mixed with olives from who knows where by those crooks in Callas," Thierry went on.

"Mais non," Chantal said. "Taste."

I had brought a small bottle of oil and poured it into two white ramekins Chantal brought out from the sideboard. She put fresh thyme in another ramekin and sea salt in a fourth. So Thierry cut slices of bread with a straight-edged knife directly on the massive oak dining table. (By using a straight-edged knife and not a bread knife, Thierry was demonstrating how well he sharpened his knives.) We dipped the bread first in the oil, then in the thyme, then in the salt and ate.

"*Eat ease not bad,*" Thierry pronounced in English, smacking his lips.

"It has the bitter taste of the hillside," Chantal said. "Yumm!"

"I think I can taste my sweat," Albert said, and we laughed.

"But I think it does not have the savor of Alexis's *petits ribiers,*" Thierry said.

"Let's not talk about Alexis," Albert said.

Chantal announced that the boar leg, which she had marinated for twenty-four hours in wine and olive oil and slowly roasted all afternoon, was ready.

"I have made something very special for you, Ken," she said. "Do you know what is *pipérade?*"

I thought it was an omelet from the Pays Basque—at least, that's where I had heard the term before.

"No," she said. "In Provence, *pipérade* is a stew made with olive oil and garlic and different-colored peppers. You will see."

When she had brought the main dishes to the table and we were all seated, I held out my hands.

"You will say *ze zhank-you* now?" Thierry said.

"If you agree?"

"But of course!"

I thanked God for the blessings of this year. I thanked God for the blessings of wonderful and plentiful food, and for this place. I thanked God for friendship. And I thanked him for his greatest gift of all: our freedom.

"And don't let the Socialists take it away from us," I concluded.

"Amen!" they all shouted, and then laughed.

The boar was cooked perfectly. Chantal had successfully tenderized the normally tough, dry meat with the marinade, and while it didn't fall away from the bone—wild boar never does, except in stew—Thierry was able to cut thin slices that we slathered with *pipérade*. It

was magnificent, and we continued with the Peyrassol, which paired nicely with it.

"I don't understand why you go all the way to Callas to press your olives," Thierry said, after we had all eaten a bit.

"That's where Alexis goes. Where else is there?"

"If you did everything Alexis did, you would not still be happily married," Thierry said.

"Let's not talk about Alexis," Albert said.

"Where else is there?" I asked again.

"You did not know? There is a new olive mill right next door in Grimaud."

"Where?" I asked.

"As you come down the road from La Garde-Freinet, there is a sign on the left just before the village."

That was news to me—and very good news. Callas was an hour away. This new mill in Grimaud couldn't be more than twenty minutes.

"You should try it for next year's harvest. It is run by a young farmer, who has olives himself."

Mentally, I made a note. "I will," I said.

"Alexis has a new girlfriend," Chantal said.

"Do we really have to talk about Alexis?" Albert said.

"She's Ukrainian," said Thierry. "Tall. Blonde. Slav."

He drew her body in the air with great relish.

"She is very nice," Chantal said, with a definitive air. "Her name is Galina. She is hoping Alexis will sponsor her green card."

"Good luck with that," Albert said.

"She does everything for him," Chantal said. "What's the harm? She's not looking for his money. She just wants a chance to come to Europe."

"She wouldn't be the first," I said. "What does that tell you about a society where the women are ready to sell themselves as sex slaves to escape?"

I got to meet Galina many months later, and she truly was a remarkable young woman—much too good for Alexis, I thought. But then, so were most of the women he courted. Except for one—and she would get the better of him in the end.

Pruning

That winter, I attacked the olives in earnest. Christina and I skied at Limone, Italy, in late January, and then she returned to the States and I bought a rototiller and began clearing stumps from the terraces. If you have ever seen advertisement videos of rototillers, it looks so easy. Just put the thing in gear and it digs effortlessly into soft, rich dirt. But here, even in winter, the ground was hard and mostly stones. When I tried to go forward, the blades just skipped over the earth. So I had to dig in reverse, often getting hung up in roots or stones and creating giant pits in the earth, which I'd have to fill in.

After digging around the first couple of trees, it was clear I could not use the rototiller on the entire terrace because the area was simply too vast—nearly four acres. So I focused on digging around the trees so I could lay the nets more easily come harvest time. It was hard work. I probably lost ten pounds in ten days.

Next came the pruning. Albert had agreed to teach me what he had learned over the years helping Alexis.

"Since olive trees only produce every other year, that's when you prune them," he said.

"Maybe they only produce every other year *because* you prune them."

"What do I know?" he said. "It's what Alexis has always said."

"I thought you didn't want to talk about Alexis?"

119

"Who's talking about Alexis?" he said, pretending to be in a huff. "I was talking about pruning."

I had such a wide variety of trees that pruning was a challenge. Each tree had to be approached differently. Some grew straight and tall and had large trunks. These needed to be topped so we could harvest them efficiently. Others were smaller regrowths, with multiple main trunks, whose branches draped down at the end like a weeping willow. The basic principle, according to the books I read, was to select the main carrying branches—called *charpentières*—and cut away the others. This was called the *taille de formation*, the heavy formative work that would give structure to the tree to come. Every two years after that, you were supposed to clear the center of the tree and thin out the branches, never removing more than one-quarter of the foliage. When done correctly, a bird was supposed to be able to fly through the branches. It was a bit like raising children, instilling moral principles and applying careful discipline to wall off bad habits, always with an eye to the long view. And like raising children, it required faith. No matter how bad things might look at any given moment, you had to believe they would turn out for the best.

One morning, I took a break from my new Iran book and discovered a half-dozen olive trees up by the cistern, in a wild part of the hillside inaccessible from any road. They still had pink plastic tubes around the trunks to protect them from the boar, a sign they had been planted by careful hands many years ago. But they hadn't been pruned in thirty years.

So far, in all my wanderings up on the hillside, I had never encountered another person. But they were there. As Thierry liked to remind me, there were more people on my hillside than I would ever imagine. And not all of them were happy to see an American in this place.

Le Pipe

The next couple of months were crazy with work. I was constantly on the road with the lawyers, meeting with potential witnesses in our Iran 9/11 case in Europe and the States, and traveling with one of them to Dubai on a wild goose chase to acquire photos of Osama bin Laden in Iran.[6]

But by the end of June, we had finished the first phase of the work, and I flew back to Les Sources. The tourists hadn't yet descended on the Côte, the cicadas were singing, and the nights were long and balmy. Paradise.

Alexis invited me to dinner before Christina and the children arrived, and since it was still light out and hot at 8:00 p.m., I decided to walk. It was actually quicker to walk to his house than to drive. When I got past the neighbor's pool, a dog came down from the hamlet where Alexis lived and started barking. It was a yellow mutt, with a small head and an ugly pointed nose and sharp-looking teeth, and its bark was not friendly. I was used to dogs and extended my free hand down to my knees, inviting, but he kept his distance, barking viciously. I crossed the stone bridge and approached the first house when the dog came silently from behind and bit into the meaty part of my calf and ran off. I had never been bitten by a dog, and it was a shock.

---

[6] See *The Iran House*, chapter 25, "The CIA Drops the Ball."

I was wearing shorts, and the blood from the puncture wounds began dribbling down my leg.

"Hey-oh!" someone called.

An older man emerged from the house, a half-bent pipe stuck in his teeth. He was wearing baggy trousers and a plaid shirt with the sleeves rolled up. He walked with a slight stoop and had a graying mustache. This must be "Le Pipe," I thought. Alexis spoke of him often with derision.

He shouted at the dog and told it to get back in the house, but it ran away instead.

"Let's see what happened to you," he said apologetically.

His wife came out next. She had gray stringy hair and was also dressed in loose work clothes. She had large bags under her eyes and her skin was gray, as if she had been a lifelong drinker and smoker. She fussed over me and then offered to clean me up.

"I am a nurse," she said.

"It's more of a shock than anything else," I said.

"No, no. Let me clean you up. You don't want to get an infection."

And so I followed them to the sitting area in the shade of a mulberry tree overlooking the stream, while she went back inside to get Betadine and wipes.

"I was heading up to Alexis's house for dinner," I said.

"Ah, Alexis," he sighed. "You should have called ahead of time and we would have kept the dogs inside. He has never done this before."

I didn't know Le Pipe's real name and certainly didn't have his number, so how could I have called? But I let that slide.

"It's okay, really," I said.

His wife put a bandage over the wound and told me to take it off tomorrow and clean it again.

"Has the dog been vaccinated for rabies?" I asked.

"We don't have rabies in France," Le Pipe said.

"Really?"

"It disappeared thirty years ago."

"All the same," I said, "it would be nice to know that the dog has been vaccinated."

"Yes, of course," he said.

What he meant was not that the dog had been vaccinated, but that my concern was misplaced.

When I finally made it up to Alexis's place, he was waiting for me beneath the pergola where he normally ate, wearing a ruffled shirt open to show the white hair on his chest. The Saint-Tropez look.

"Ah, Le Pipe!" he said when I had explained what happened.

Alexis had filed any number of lawsuits against Le Pipe and talked about them frequently. He accused his neighbor of encroaching on his property to build his pool. He accused him of encroaching on his property to build a carport. He accused him of siphoning off water, of dropping rocks onto the roof of the house adjoining that of Le Pipe's that Alexis rented out. As far as I could tell, he never went to court and never won, but he kept on filing suits nonetheless. I recounted to him what one of the lawyers I worked for liked to say: a bad settlement is worth a good lawsuit. But he just scoffed.

Galina joined us from the kitchen.

"*Chéri*," she said. "You should not talk about Le Pipe. It makes your heart to beat," she said, in approximate French.

Alexis sighed with pleasure. "No, dearest. It's only you that makes my heart to beat," he said.

When he wanted to, I suppose he could actually be charming—or almost.

I started chatting with Galina in English, which she spoke with greater ease than French. She became animated and talked about her life in Paris, the small Ukrainian community, and how she hoped to get her green card so she could enroll at the Sorbonne. The longer we spoke, the more agitated Alexis became.

"Stop talking, penguin," he said harshly to both of us.

"Mais non, Alexis," I said smoothly. "It's not penguin—it's *pigeon*."

"Penguin. Pigeon. We are in France. We speak French," he said in a huff.

Alexis had a medical degree, which made him a member of the privileged classes. Ignorance was not something he could admit, especially if it put him at a disadvantage with a member of the under-class—an immigrant!—he was supposed to master. That's when I knew for sure that he couldn't speak or understand a word of English, and that it embarrassed him.

The Sailing Club

The day after Christina arrived with Simon and Diana, we drove down to Sainte-Maxime to enroll them in summer classes at the sailing club, as we did every year. This was now their fourth season, and they knew almost everyone who worked there and many of the kids their own age.

Sailing club is a fancy term for the roadside facility a kilometer up the coast road from the beaches and cafés and marina downtown.

It had a small office and social area and a cinderblock structure with showers and changing rooms. Beyond that were hangars for windsurfers, Lasers, and Optimists, the bucket-size boat used to initiate the children to the art of sailing. The largest boats were four-person catamarans. Check your yachts, dress whites, and black pearls at the door. This was serious fun.

The club was set up as a nonprofit in the 1960s in a pair of garden sheds that could be taken apart and stored over winter. Now they had a contract with the local schools and allowed visitors like Simon and Diana to enroll in the sailing classes for a nominal fee. Their teacher, Manu, was in his mid-twenties and tall, well built, and bronzed as a god, but never seemed to look in the mirror as others might. He was modest and soft-spoken and loved working with the kids. He and another instructor would sit them down for an hour in front of a whiteboard and teach them the correct angle of attack for each type of wind, and then accompany them on the water in Zodiacs, where they learned how to capsize their boats and right them. In all the summers we spent there, we never once heard a whining child or a complaining parent.

One afternoon, when we went to pick up Simon and Diana, there was a group of adults in the commons, glasses in hand. So we went in.

"Ah, Madame Timmerman, monsieur," said Catherine, the club secretary, so others could hear. "We were just about to have our monthly cocktail. Come join us."

And so we did.

All the talk was about the star graduates of the club: Olivier Bausset and Jean-Baptiste Bernaz. They were in training for the 2008 Olympic Games. Bausset was the grandson of the founder of the club, so his name rolled off local tongues with particular pride.

Inevitably, once Catherine announced that I was a writer and war correspondent, someone asked me about politics.

"The war in Iraq is not going well," one man said.

"No, it's not," I conceded. "It was never the plan to occupy the country. But that's what we've done, with entirely predictable results."

"We feel very sorry for the families of those American soldiers who have been killed to free Iraq," another man said.

This was a far cry from the type of thing I heard in Paris when I went to interview politicians and appear on French television. The TV hosts invariably introduced me as a "Bush supporter," not as an author or a correspondent for the *Washington Times*, where I then worked. I can't imagine even CNN bringing on a reporter from *Le Monde* and introducing them as a "Chirac supporter," but hey, who's counting.

"Thank you," I said. "Things have changed a lot since Vietnam. Many of these young men joined the military after 9/11. They are patriotic and their families are patriotic and we celebrate them as heroes."

We had several glasses of champagne with the group while the kids were having fruit juice up on the balcony with Manu and the other instructors. Catherine was telling Christina about her husband, who had just left her. When I joined them, she turned to me.

"I've got to set up a dinner so you can meet my husband," she said.

"I thought you had just separated," I said, perplexed.

"Oh, we have. But we still talk."

Her husband had worked for a French defense company and had been in Iraq just before the outbreak of the war, so she figured we had probably crossed paths.

"So why did he leave you and the children?" I wondered. It was the type of question you could ask in France without being impertinent or impolite.

"He started thinking too much," she said. Then, out of the blue, she added: "You really should write a book about your experiences. People would find it fascinating."

I had never considered that before, sticking to the mantra I had learned from decades of field reporting that you don't become the subject of your own stories. But as I toyed with the idea, I thought a good way to start would be by telling the story of how Christina and I came to return to France, just nine years after the French government tried to kick me out for being a spy.

Which, of course, I was not—at least, not in the way they thought I was.

So thank you, Catherine.[7]

Christina turned to me in the car on the way home.

"You didn't get it, did you?"

"Get what?"

"Catherine."

"I thought she was very gracious."

"About her husband."

"Sure. She wants to get him back."

"He's probably off with some secretary who is twenty years younger," Christina said.

"Would you want me back if I did something like that?"

I knew the answer, of course. But I liked to hear her say it.

"If I ever caught you—"

"Sshh!" I hissed. "The children!"

---

[7] I originally planned to layer in my experiences as a war correspondent, of being taken hostage and tortured in Lebanon, and literally being born again in the ashes of a Beirut cellar, but set those stories aside for a separate memoir, *And the Rest Is History: Tales of Hostages, Arms Dealers, Dirty Tricks, and Spies.* A follow-on volume, *The Iran House*, details my involvement in an Israeli government effort to help the Iranian opposition overthrow the Islamic regime, among other tales.

But when I looked in the rearview mirror, they were sound asleep, their heads resting against each other. And Christina was grinning like she had just eaten a mouse.

Le Club 55

Le Club Cinquante-Cinq was not a club, and few people knew what the "55" referred to, but it was as famous as the Pampelonne beach where it was located. When a certain category of person thought of Saint-Tropez, the images conjured in their mind were of this beach and of this eatery shaded beneath tamarisk trees and huge white umbrellas where guests eyed each other surreptitiously wondering who was rich and famous.

And what was that category of person? Certainly not us. The irony of it was that neither the beach nor the restaurant were actually in Saint-Tropez but in neighboring Ramatuelle. But if you were a *midinette*—the French term for that category of person who aspired to the imagined glamour of others—it simply wouldn't do to say you had summered in Ramatuelle. It sounded in French like a supplementary health insurance program. And who wanted to be called a *Ramatuelloise*? Much better to go as a *Tropezienne*, which was also a famous cream pastry.

That July was the first time in our four years in the area that we actually ate lunch at the Club Cinquante-Cinq. As it happened, we were invited as fools to the king and queen of Sweden at a gathering thrown in their honor by a friend of ours.

Among the Swedes who lived or summered in the south of France, it was a well-kept secret that the royal family regularly spent one or two months in Sainte-Maxime at the house of Prince Bertil, the king's uncle. Bertil was outgoing and personable, known for his love of fast cars and boats. The town had even named one of the parking lots in the marina after him because he loved to play *pétanque* there with the locals. When Christina and I went to the pebble beach by the sailing camp, we sat directly facing Bertil's villa, which was on the promontory before entering town. If the king was in residence, security guards would patrol the waters at the back of the house on Jet Skis, and you could see them also by the front gates on the coast road. Sometimes, the king would bring up his low-slung mahogany speedboat and anchor it just behind the villa. It stood out because it was painted robin's egg blue. And when he lunched at the Club Cinquante-Cinq, as today, he would anchor in the bay where all the rich and famous left their boats. The club had a dinghy to fetch guests from their yachts to a private wharf. Okay, it wasn't really a dinghy but a twin-engine boat that could carry sixteen people. And the tractor they used to groom the beach was a Lamborghini. No joke.

Our friend Matthias, who was the host, was a fabulously successful businessman who had introduced big Swedish brands to China and wound up investing early in Shanghai real estate. By the time of this lunch, his real estate holdings in China dwarfed his commercial business, and he spoke fluent Mandarin. They had purchased and renovated an old farmhouse around fifteen minutes above us in the mountains. Surrounded by trees, it looked out over the vast wilderness of the Var outside of La Garde-Freinet. They had installed marble floors, central heating, a large patio, and a deep pool. We had been to their place a few times for dinners and they were always gracious hosts, as we tried to be when they visited us.

But Matthias was bored with his money. Now, he was more interested in following the Swedish king on the hunting and leisure circuit. The hunting piece of it began in mid-August in Sörmland, rolling farmlands and forests just south of Stockholm, when the season on buck deer opened. Then they traveled north in late August to hunt the *ripa*, a special kind of grouse that was only found in Lapland near the Arctic Circle. In October, they choppered up to a hunting lodge owned by another wealthy friend of the king to hunt elk. In the summers, they all tramped down to the Côte d'Azur, the king with his entourage and Matthias with his credit card. As Matthias explained, that was what friends were for.

Matthias invited us to the lunch the night before.

"He must have been going through his guest list and found it a bit thin," I remarked. "It's gutsy on his part to invite someone like me for lunch with the king."

"You'll behave," Christina said. "Just don't drink too much."

"I'll keep an eye on him," Steve said. He and his wife, Shoshana Bryen, were our best friends in Maryland and were visiting us after attending a board meeting in Rome. We had asked Matthias if they could join us, and he was overjoyed to have a former senior Pentagon official—someone with a title!—join the party. They thought it would be fun. Steve, whose first wife was Swedish, even claimed to recall a few words in Swedish, although I doubted that would be necessary. Queen Silvia, who was half Brazilian, was known to be a skilled linguist and proficient in six languages.

We packed into Steve's rental car for the forty-five-minute drive to the Ramatuelle beaches and the Boulevard Patch that led to the Club Cinquante-Cinq, since my ten-year-old Golf GTI was a bit long in the tooth to leave at the valet parking. (Yes, I could get embarrassed by our *voiture de coiffeuse*, but Simon loved the sound the engine made. It reminded him of the Rallye du Var....)

For the record, the "55" simply refers to the year the owners, Geneviève et Bernard de Colmont, established the restaurant as the unofficial canteen for the actors, producers, and technicians making Roger Vadim's epoch-making film, *Et Dieu Créa La Femme* (*And God Created Woman*). This was the film that announced the sexual revolution and launched the career of Brigitte Bardot as a "sex kitten," as the movie critics called her. It was also the film that made Saint-Tropez famous.

For all the snootiness and pretention of the clientele, the de Colmont family prided themselves on serving honest fare at relatively decent prices, given the surroundings. They branded their own rosé from the local *cave coopérative* and usually had a *plat de jour* from between fifteen to twenty euros. As I learned later, you needed to call ahead the day before to snag a table.

Matthias had reserved three tables for us, off in a secluded corner close to the beach. As we stood around and mingled before sitting down to eat, I tried to get a feel for the other guests, but couldn't. Matthias and Annika were going over the seating arrangement, and everyone seemed to be self-conscious in the presence of the king, who was wearing a light green polo shirt and a knitted beanie—to disguise himself in case there were paparazzi about.

We had only one choice to make as far as the menu was concerned: salmon or grilled meat as a main course. Everything else was set ahead of time. The meal was pleasant, and as the wine began to loosen tongues, we started to feel comfortable with our tablemates. Steve, now the president-CEO of the US subsidiary of Finmeccanica, the giant Italian defense conglomerate, was in his element. He

was a formidable cook and entertained them with stories of Italian food and wine. He and Shoshana were far more accomplished conversationalists than I was with complete strangers.

As we waited for dessert, people got up and mingled again. Annika went off to one side with Queen Silvia, who had been talking with Steve about his daughter Gabrielle. She was a US Army officer serving in Iraq. The queen was very interested in women soldiers.

Annika motioned for me to come over.

"Ken is a prominent Iran expert in the United States," she said.

The queen shook my hand and didn't miss a beat.

"We have many Iranians living in Sweden. Should we really be afraid of Iran?"

"You do have many Iranians living in Sweden," I said. "And the overwhelming majority of them came to Sweden to escape the Islamic state of Iran, whether they are monarchists who came right after the revolution or Kurds who have come more recently. These Iranians are your friends and your allies. It's the regime you need to be worried about."

"So do you think we should do business with Iran?" she asked. "Matthias and his friends are convinced that we should. What do you think?"

"The Iranian regime is dangerous. And it is evil," I said. "When I speak to business groups, I tell them that if they trade with Iran, they will get AIDS."

"What do you mean?"

"Sooner or later, their shameful business will be exposed, and they will regret sacrificing their good name for a small profit."

"But why is it shameful to do business with Iran? I have always thought of Persia as a great country with a millennial culture."

"It is. But the Islamic regime has perverted Iran. If you are a woman living in Iran today, you can be stoned to death if your husband accuses you of adultery. You cannot leave the country without his written permission. Young girls can be forced to marry at the age of twelve."

I sensed that the queen had heard all this, so I took another tack. "The International Atomic Energy Agency is now debating whether to put sanctions on Iran because it has maintained a clandestine nuclear weapons program for the past twenty years. Just imagine what a fanatical regime could do with nuclear weapons."

"That would be horrible, of course. But how do we know for sure they are building nuclear weapons?"

"We don't," I said. "We never can, until they explode a bomb. And that's the problem. Rafsanjani, their president, talked about a nuclear war with Israel in a public speech a few years ago. He said that such a thing was possible, and if it happened, Iran would lose millions of people. But Israel would cease to exist."

The queen gave an involuntary shiver. She was born in Nazi Germany toward the end of World War II to a wealthy German industrialist. I had no idea of her feelings about Israel, but the thought of another Holocaust seemed to affect her.

"How can he talk about mass murder in such a way?"

"He's not the only one. That's why I always believe in listening to what they say. If they say they want to kill you, you should take them at their word."

After dessert and coffee, the king and queen departed. Exactly how, I'm not sure. One minute they were there, and the next they were gone, whisked away by the security guards who had been watching them discreetly all afternoon.

We took Steve and Shoshana to the crowded beach just beyond the restaurant and swam in the pale green water out to the anchored boats. When the sun declined, I suggested we drive to Saint-Tropez to look at the big boats in the harbor. Steve found one he liked and posed for pictures in front of it. It was a three-deck, 167-foot beauty called *Alibi*.

We rarely go to Saint-Tropez, but when we do, it's usually at sunset, since the harbor faces due west and remains hot and lit well after the beaches. If you aren't worried about being seen—which requires taking a front-row seat at Le Sénéquier or another of the harbor-side

cafés—then I suggest you do as we did that evening and enter the alleyway after the Café de Paris and go up the staircase to the Hôtel Sube. They have the best bar in town, full of ship's lanterns and English leather armchairs and old nautical gear, and a tiny balcony where you can watch the sun set over the mountains and the crowded street scene and yachts below. They have excellent white wine from a local châteaux and champagne in "swimming pool" glasses. And, if you come early, stop by the Musée de l'Annonciade, which has an astonishing collection of Bonnards. As the French say, they are worth the *détour*.

A Jew from Alexandria[8]

When I was alone in the house and writing, as I was again that autumn waiting for Christina to join me for the olive harvest, I often felt like a monk. And it wasn't just for the obvious reason. The house was stark and bare, with white walls and ceilings set off by dark wooden beams and, upstairs in my writing room, by a wall of sober stones above the fireplace. Most of the light fixtures looked like ancient candle sconces, and in the dining room where I spent time in winter I was flanked by copies of Renaissance tapestries and simple silver candelabra and the graven stone plaque set in a recess with the date 1099 in Roman numerals. In the staircase up to my study was an eighteen-inch Madonna on a stone shelf. I felt like I was in a monastery, for real. All that was lacking was the murmuring of the Jesus Prayer. Sometimes I murmured it myself, alternating between French and English.[9]

My work schedule was as monastic as the house itself. I would wake up early and walk the hillside for an hour before breakfast. Then I would write all morning, take a simple lunch, and do physical work in the afternoon. I never went to restaurants alone—I had enough of that when I was on the road. And we did not join the social circle in

---

[8] A tribute to Per Ahlmark, 1939–2018.

[9] Lord Jesus Christ, Son of God, have mercy on me, a sinner. Seigneur Jésus, Fils de Dieu, aie pitié de moi, pêcheur.

our village, except for the friends I had made. But every morning when I awoke, I felt blessed and praised the Lord for my good fortune and his bounty. This was my earthly paradise. I was happy to be a monk.

Before Christina arrived, a friend of ours from Stockholm, Per Ahlmark, came to visit. It was not exactly the tourist season, so I was intrigued when he phoned to see if he could fly down for a few days. He had a

new project he wanted to discuss with me. I was happy to have company but insisted that I would keep to my normal work schedule.

He arrived at the airport with a large roll-on and a checked bag so heavy that he had to pay excess baggage fees.

"What in the world have you got in these things?" I asked as I hefted them onto a cart.

Per gave me a leprechaun grin. "I asked Elie Wiesel the same question when he came to visit me. He said: 'It's watermelons, I can't possibly travel without them.' So these are my watermelons. All of your books, for one thing."

If you come to visit an author carrying his books, you are bound to make a friend, if you weren't one already. Per's project involved Iran.

"I want to do something extraordinary," he said over dinner the first night. "And you and your friend John Bolton are at the very center of my plan. I want to nominate the two of you for the Nobel Peace Prize."

"You're joking," I said.

"No, I am deadly serious. And I need your help, because I don't know Ambassador Bolton."

As a former Swedish member of parliament and deputy prime minister, Per was legally entitled to submit nominations to the Nobel Committee—unlike people like Richard Holbrooke, who reportedly tried to nominate himself. As Per walked me through his idea, it began to seem less far-fetched. The Nobel Committee had felt that Iran's nuclear weapons program was dangerous enough to award the Peace Prize that year jointly to the International Atomic Energy Agency (IAEA) and to its director general, Mohamed ElBaradei. And yet, Per argued, for eighteen years the IAEA had done nothing to inhibit Iran's nuclear ambitions, despite mounting evidence that Iran was using its civilian nuclear program as a legend for acquiring the equipment and the know-how to build the bomb.

"So, if they are so concerned about Iran to award the prize to the toothless watchdog of Vienna, they should award next year's prize to two people who have actually done something about it: you, for having provided the first early warning, and Ambassador Bolton, for his work at the State Department to block shipments of dangerous technology from reaching Iran," Per said.[10]

Per was a witty and often acerbic columnist, known as a passionate defender of Israel and the United States. In a country that still paid lip service to public intellectuals, he was respected by many and feared by those who held opposing views. At sixty-six, he retained a hint of the rakishness that had attracted Swedish film star Bibi Andersson twenty years earlier, with a Peer Gynt profile and steely blue eyes that could turn water to ice and back again. (He and the star of many Ingmar Bergman films were married for two years but stayed together only one.) And yet, he had a physical awkwardness that could be almost painful. When I was cooking, he wanted to help but managed to put himself in exactly the wrong place so that I nearly ran into him every time I turned from the stove. He was intense and

---

[10] See Per Ahlmark, "Let the Nobel Go Nuclear," *Wall Street Journal*, February 7, 2006. https://www.wsj.com/articles/SB113927966131966843. Ambassador Bolton's program to interdict shipments at sea was called the Counter Proliferation Initiative, and he had convinced more than a dozen US allies in Europe and Asia to join it.

wound up. I hoped the time in the olive orchard would help him to decompress.

Being a friend of Israel in Sweden did not come easily, but Per had never wavered in his support for the Jewish state. Ironically, all of the many illnesses and accidents that had befallen him in recent years had happened during trips to Israel. One year, he had a stroke. Another, he caught pneumonia. During a third, just recently, he tore his Achilles tendon while walking—so I couldn't take him, as I would have liked, hiking up my hillside or on the rocks at the Cap Taillat.

"In another life, I was a Jew from Alexandria," he said. "I am not a Viking. I hate the cold." Even when the sun came out, he wrapped himself in a heavy wool scarf, a sweater, and a long, heavy coat.

The first night he was here, I said grace before we sat down to a *pot au feu*. I read parts of the 94th Psalm—up until verse eleven: "The Lord knows the thoughts of man; he knows that they are futile." This comes after several verses where the psalmist implores God to punish his enemies and to "pay back to the proud what they deserve."

Because of his love for Israel, I had just assumed that Per was a believer. He listened to the psalm keenly, and to me, it seemed that it spoke to him. But it was only as we talked over the next two days

that he revealed he had always considered himself an agnostic, at best, and began his political career at the age of sixteen by opposing the Swedish state church.

"I even traveled to Vienna to get married the first time," he said, "because it was the most secular place in Europe."

So I prayed less with him, but I talked about my faith, and, in particular, my belief that God had a plan for each one of us—one for me, one for Per, one for Christina, one for every person that we knew. Clearly, it puzzled him, but I sensed he was intrigued. After all, God's plan had brought the two of us together for this quixotic assault on the Nobel Committee.

It rained heavily for two days. I continued to write in the mornings, but instead of harvesting olives in the afternoons, I took Per to tour the countryside. One day, after lunch in Saint-Tropez, he talked about his three marriages, which he had ruined because he could never fully commit to another person. It wasn't the ex-wives he regretted, however. It was a relationship long ago with a Swedish Jewess, who committed suicide just as he was poised to become prime minister at age thirty-six.

"I completely lost my hunger for politics when she died," he said. "None of it made sense any longer. My obsession with my political career had totally blinded me to her pain. I announced I was resigning my position, and from politics altogether, at the very party conference where they were planning to anoint me as party leader. Everyone was shocked and begged me to reconsider. But I have never regretted that decision, and I have never gone back to politics."

"Maybe in your pain God was speaking to you," I suggested. "He sets us horrible trials to test us and to find his own."

The day before Per was scheduled to return to Stockholm, the mistral began to blow, so I phoned Albert to see if he could help me harvest the olives before the wind destroyed the crop. He looked like a peasant, his features sharp and as dark as an old saddle. Per watched us maneuver the nets around the trees and occasionally tried to rake a branch, without much success.

We broke for lunch up at the house, and I said a brief grace of thanksgiving over red wine. I ended by combining a secular toast among friends with a hint of the Eucharist: "Drink of this often—and I do—and every time you drink of it think of friendship, love, and the goodness of the Lord."

Per turned to Albert in utter seriousness: "So has he convinced you that God is good, and that he is watching?"

"Absolutely," Albert said.

"He's starting to convince me, too," said Per.

Deliverance

Christina arrived from Washington, DC, just after Per left, and we finished the olives together. The weather had cleared, and in the bright sunshine, the colors were astonishing. On a single tree—even on a single branch—the olives ranged from light green to violet to dark black. This was the stage of ripeness called *tournant*, when the color was changing. Most people I had spoken with considered this to be the best moment to harvest the fruit. Too early, and it was too bitter. Too late, and it lost its pungency and pepper. Some of the trees were so heavily laden with fruit that the branches drooped to the ground, and we had to empty the nets repeatedly because they were so heavy. The olives festooned the branches like garlands of jewels.

We harvested the smaller trees from the ground, but for the older trees, I had to climb up the trunks or reach them on a ladder. Christina hated this, because it was precarious business. You needed two hands to harvest: one to hold the branch, the second to comb the leaves, so it was a constant balancing act. I don't know how many times I felt myself swaying and had to grab hold of the trunk to keep from falling. And then you had to position the ladder on boards so the feet wouldn't poke holes in the net. If it slipped, you went down.

"It's not worth killing yourself," she said repeatedly.

"I have no intention of killing myself," I said.

"If the branch is too high, just cut it off."

She had a point—what else were those branches for but to bear olives for the harvest? But I was new to this, and I couldn't bear to bring violence to these trees that had responded with such abundance to the care I had shown them. Besides, there was a particular pleasure in grasping a frond bursting with olives and raking it onto the metal steps of the ladder. *Pling-pling-pl-pl-pl-plingggg.* What a sound! Like pieces of silver being dropped into a pouch. One large tree produced twenty-five kilos—as much as we had harvested from the entire orchard the previous year. And all of this after just two years of work, clearing the orchard, pruning the trees, fertilizing, and spraying. How bounteous was the Lord!

I had purchased six of the regulation crates when Albert and I had visited Callas last fall, and they were full after harvesting the top terrace, so I called ahead to the new olive press Thierry had told us about at Thanksgiving. Monsieur Lanza, the owner, warned me about the road.

"What kind of vehicle do you have?" he said.

"A Golf GTI."

He laughed. "You won't make it here. Or if you do, you won't make it back up. You need a 4x4."

Albert was happy to serve as my wheels, and we posed for pictures with the six crates bursting with ripe olives at the back of his gun-metal Land Rover Defender. I crouched down and ran my hands

through the olives as if they were a treasure chest of coin. And in many ways, I suppose they were. My hands had a luxurious silkiness from handling the fruit.

We came down the main road from La Garde-Freinet and over-shot the turnoff since the sign came up with no warning. The minute we turned around and hit the dirt road, I understood what Monsieur Lanza had meant.

"This is a streambed," I said. "I've been on roads in the Bekaa Valley better than this."

"Aren't you glad we didn't take your *voiture de coiffeuse*?" Albert grinned.

"No kidding," I said. "Thanks."

The road wound down, down, down through vineyards, and then around a tight curve into dense shade and old chestnut trees and brown uncut grass. At the next switchback, the grass had been cleared, and a hobbled llama was gnawing at stubble in a muddy pen. In the distance, a donkey brayed.

We bottomed out into a floodplain, luxuriant with foliage. Broken wagons and rusting farm machinery littered the high places. Ahead of us, on a slight rise, was a dilapidated stone farmhouse. A carport with a tin roof covered an ancient tractor, the type with the narrow wheelbase and high wheels used by the winegrowers. It must have been from the 1950s, with an open cab. Chickens were pecking the ground and scattered when we followed the sign to the press just beyond the house.

"This is like the movie *Deliverance*," I said. "Have you ever seen it?"

"The one with the kids in the canoe and the old pervert with no teeth?"

"Yeah. I wasn't thinking of the pervert so much as the setting. What a mess!"

Beyond an open shed that looked like an outdoor kitchen with a gas cooker and greasy shelves and stacks of dirty dishes, there was a muddy parking area with a small flatbed and a Toyota 4x4, both streaked with mud. The mud track continued beyond the buildings through scrub woods to a vineyard that sloped off into yet another hidden valley. Down, down, down. Albert backed carefully so we could unload our crates by the stacks of others waiting to be pressed.

"Is Monsieur Lanza here?" I asked the teenager who came out to help us unload.

"I'm his son, Didier. He's inside with the press."

Didier found an empty crate of the same type as mine and put it on the scale to set the *tare*; then he weighed our six crates, stacked three high.

"110.4 kilos," he said.

That was just beyond the hundred-kilo minimum for our own press run—half what we would have needed at Callas. I was excited: for the first time, we would actually have our own oil!

Beyond the scales and the stacks of olives was a glass door leading into a small room that held the press itself. It was not what I had expected. Callas was an industrial facility, the size of a cooperative wine cellar with thirty-foot ceilings and giant stainless-steel vats connected by tubes a foot in diameter. This was a farmhouse kitchen by comparison. The olives were fed into a washtub the size of a big sink, where twigs and leaves floated to the top. Then they moved to the crusher, a water trough like you'd see at any small farm but with a thick stainless-steel screw at the bottom that churned them into a light green pulp. From there, the pulp was fed into a long, horizontal, stainless-steel centrifuge with a tiny tube at the bottom that dripped pure green oil into a decantation trough. From the bottom, a small pump attached to a garden hose fed the clarified oil into clean buckets, and from there into a measuring pitcher. As the French would say, it was *artisanal*. But it worked.

Monsieur Lanza, the owner, was in his late thirties and was sweating from overwork, but he still took time to chat with us and with other clients who crowded around him at the press, eager to see their oil emerge as if from some alchemist's alembic. He spoke with the thick local accent you could cut with a spoon. His eyes lit up when I told him I was American.

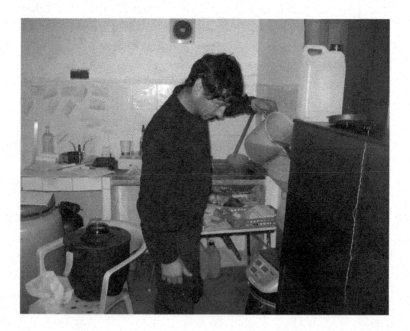

"Really? How come you speak such good French?" he said.

"Ouf. I lived here for eighteen years, mostly in Paris. I did a lot of radio and TV, so I had to speak French."

"But still. We hear Americans on TV, and they have this, uh, quaint accent."

"Monsieur Lanza is very polite," Albert laughed.

"That's true," I said. "I've always wondered about that, too."

We got to talking with an older man in rough blue work clothes, a beret, and a hunter's vest. I told him a bit about how long it took for me to discover the olives in all the underbrush. He introduced himself as Ugue.

"Where are you exactly?" Ugue asked.

When I told him, he lit up.

"That's the Drug House!" he said.

"What?"

He explained that forty years earlier, when he was a much younger man—and, of course, far more attractive to women—he had helped the local gendarmes conduct a drug raid on my house and seize a crazy amount of marijuana and hashish.

"Everybody knew Stenberg, the Swedish match king," he said. "But they also remember the summer of 1965, when he rented the villa to the heir of a famous automaker whose daughter got caught up with a young couple who kept a boat on the property. They used the boat to make round trips to Amsterdam, where they loaded hashish into secret compartments in the gunwales. Then they cruised to a private boat landing in Saint-Tropez and hauled the boat up to the house after dark."

"It sounds like *The French Connection*," Albert said.

"It was pretty big," Ugue said, happy to have an audience. "We got a tip-off from the gardener. He told us to wait until they brought the boat up to the house on its trailer. He was right."

The gendarmes had Ugue and a group of local cops block the exits.

"The villa is up on a hill, so they could escape down the other side and get away on the road to La Garde-Freinet. So I posted my boys on the road beyond the house with large flashlights. And sure enough, when the gendarmes went up the driveway, the people in the house tried to flee—and we caught them. We found the dope in the boat. But then we came back the next day and found an additional stash in a strange-shaped cupboard beneath the staircase."

"Do you remember where the cupboard was located?" I asked.

Ugue laughed. "How could I ever forget? It was in the bathroom."

"Unbelievable," I said. "That's *my* bathroom! We use it as a medicine cabinet because it's a bit hard to use for anything else. It's all angles but very deep."

"Exactly. The first time the gendarmes looked at it, they didn't find anything. I told them they should pull away the blankets and boxes and look behind. That's where we found the dope."

"So, Ken," Albert said slyly. "Have you checked to see if the gendarmes missed anything?"

"Oh, I doubt that," Ugue said. "We conducted a pretty thorough search after that. If you like, I can bring you the newspaper about the raid when you come back for your oil."

We arranged with Monsieur Lanza to come back three days later for the first batch of oil. Meanwhile, we finished the harvest and brought another six crates of olives from the lower terrace. In all, our first harvest came to 220 kilograms, nearly 500 pounds. I couldn't believe it.

Thierry wanted to come with us when we returned, since he hadn't actually visited the new mill yet.

"*Deliverance*," he said, shaking his head as we bounced down through the vineyards and passed the llama. "That's exactly what it is!"

He started talking with Monsieur Lanza about the olives and the press and quickly learned that the local government was subsidizing young farmers to go into the olive business in an effort to keep them on the land. That prospect intrigued him. Thierry liked to know how things worked, not just mechanically but also financially. André Lanza had taken up the business from his father, who was getting too old to harvest the sixty hectares of olives he owned in the area. André's olive press was as clean and neat as the rest of the farm was a mess.

Ugue soon joined us carrying a copy of *Var Matin* in a plastic document sleeve. It was dated July 29, 1965, with a banner headline:

DRUG HOUSE IN THE VAR! A SEIZURE FOR THE RECORD BOOKS!

It was the comings and goings of the boat that first attracted the attention of Martin S—, a gardener from Cogolin, the poor cousin of glamorous Saint Tropez...

The front page showed a photograph of a stealthy twin-engined motorboat on a trailer in front of a garage. *My garage!* It was unmistakable.

"*Et bien, l'Américain!*" Thierry said. "You are living in the Drug House!"

"We've called it that ever since," Ugue said. "Everybody does."

"They never mentioned a word of it to me when we bought it."

I was flummoxed, and not a little embarrassed. It was not pleasant to realize that perfect strangers had combed through every inch of a property you thought to be private, your own secret garden. But I guess it was similar to what Thierry liked to tell me about the hillside. You thought you owned it, but people were roaming across it at all hours of day and night.

Thankfully, the article had no zoom-out pictures of the house or anything in the description to identify exactly where it was. Nor did they identify the Swedish owner—only the drug-trafficking renters who had attracted the attention of the gardener because of their late-night forays to the boat landing and wild parties at the pool. *My pool.*

"I helped the gendarmes pack up the dope," Ugue said. "Just the smell of it gave me the trots!"

As we were talking, André continued to operate the olive press, and the clear green oil poured steadily into the plastic jugs he positioned beneath the centrifuge.

"This is your first harvest, monsieur?" André asked me as he did the paperwork to check out our oil.

"The first real harvest," I said. "Last year, I hadn't yet cleared the terraces."

"Two hundred twenty-five kilos. That's good work!" he said.

"I'm thinking of planting more trees. Is there any particular variety I should get?"

"The *tanche* and *picholine* are the standards around here. But it doesn't matter much, since almost all of the olives you buy from the nurseries are self-pollinating."

"I'll remember that," I said.

We piled back into Albert's Land Rover and drove back to my place, where Christina welcomed us with crisp fresh bread and ramekins of salt and herbs, and of course, several bottles of cold rosé from Canta Rainette—the Singing Frog.

"So, let us see how is zees American olive oil," Thierry said.

"It's not really American," Albert said. "Just made by an American."

"In part," I said.

Thierry dipped a teaspoon in the oil, sniffed it, and then rolled the teaspoon on his tongue.

"It is fruity, a bit peppery. Ha! This is almost as good as Alexis's oil," he pronounced.

"It is much better than Alexis's oil," Albert said. "It is *généreux*"—a double entendre meaning rich as well as generous.

"That's better than *générale*," I said.

"Which general?" Thierry said.

"General Motors," Albert said.

"I've had wine in Maryland that tasted like motor oil—too much clay in the soil."

"Here, you only have *shit* in the soil," Thierry said. Pronounced *sheet*, it was French slang for hashish.

It didn't take long, but with the new oil, salt, herbs, and the wine, soon we all became singing frogs.

Bouillie Bordelaise

The following year, the olives were a bust. And it was all my own fault.

Albert picked me up at the Nice airport in late March. I had carved out three weeks to work on a novel about Iran that was a fictional projection of the investigation I had been doing for the lawyers on the 9/11 attacks. I wrote in the mornings, worked in the olive orchard or cleared brush in the afternoon, and did research for the next day's writing in the late afternoons or early evenings.[11]

I broke the monastic lifestyle by occasional outings with Albert or dinners with Thierry and Chantal.

"What do you know about *bouillie bordelaise?*" I asked Albert one day.

This was a farmer's remedy for just about everything that ailed olives, grapes, and other cash crops. I had heard that it prevented rot and many insect attacks.

"Not much," he said. "But it's very common."

It was common, and available in our local Bricolage store. So I bought a bag of it and sprayed the blue slurry on the trees in the third week of April, just as they were starting to flower.

---

[11] Kenneth Timmerman, *Honor Killing* (Cassiopeia Press, 2007). http://kentimmerman.com/honor-killing.htm.

When I returned in June, the flowers had shriveled without form-ing olives. And then I looked in the research section of the olive book I had bought in Callas. While they recommended an early spring application to ward off a variety of ailments, the words leapt off the page: "*Jamais sur les fleurs!*"

The copper in the mixture was fatal to olives during pollination. Better to get the *oeil de paon*, a sickness that turned the leaves brittle and made them fall than apply the *bouillie bordelaise* on the flowers. Lesson learned.

I was doing a lot of transatlantic travel that year, not just to Europe, but also to Israel, to cover the war with Hezbollah.[12] So when I got ready to return to Les Sources in mid-October to continue work on the novel, I thought I would try a homeopathic remedy for jet lag. Shortly after takeoff from Washington, DC, I took melatonin. The result? I didn't sleep a wink during the whole flight or even on the connecting flight to Nice.

---

[12] Kenneth Timmerman, "War Tourists," in *The Iran House*, forthcoming.

The next day, Albert was heading up to Paris to see a girlfriend, so I drove him to the train station at Les Arcs in the morning and then decided to walk around the medieval city. Les Arcs was famous as the home of Saint Roseline, the devout daughter of the local nobleman who took pity on the village poor. Every evening, she would sneak out the back door of the castle and distribute the day's leftovers to the needy. Her father became suspicious and surprised her one evening just as she was going outside. He asked her what she had hidden in the folds of her dress. After a moment's hesitation, she said: "Roses." He made her drop the folds, expecting to see the food she'd been taking from the table fall to the cobblestone. Instead, out came a torrent of roses. She soon entered a convent and became Mother Superior and later was beatified on the basis of the "miracle of the roses." The nearby Chapelle Sainte Roseline is now a winery and tourist stop, with glorious Marc Chagall mosaics and stained-glass windows commissioned by art dealer Maguerite Maeght. But the castle itself is less well known, and the steep cobbled streets of the old town with their twists and turns and hidden fountains are magical.

Walking up along the castle walls, I started to feel dizzy. An overwhelming sense of fatigue swept over me. As I turned a corner near the top, I felt I was about to fall asleep on my feet and leaned against a wall to steady myself.

Next thing I knew, I was looking up into the faces of two paramedics, with a significant pain in my right thigh. I must have blacked out. For a moment, I didn't know where I was. My head felt like a slurry of *bouillie bordelaise*. A well-dressed woman, looking very concerned as she floated over me, spoke in English. "Sir, do you know where you are?"

I had a moment of panic. I *thought* I had just arrived in France on an airplane. Why was this person speaking to me in English? Was I back in the States? What had happened to me? Where was I?

Seeing my confusion, the paramedics asked me in French if I knew who I was, and I said yes, of course, I did.

"Why is she speaking to me in English?" I asked. "Are you trying to confound me?"

I wanted to walk back to my car and head home and sleep for the rest of the day, but they insisted on packing me into an ambulance and taking me to the local hospital. They ran an EKG and did blood work, thinking I had had a heart attack or possibly a blood clot. They did an MRI from my neck to my chest and still found nothing, so eventually, they released me at 4:30 p.m.

Making matters worse, I had left my phone in my car and now had no easy way of getting back to it from the hospital, which was several miles away. In the end, I took a bus into Draguignan and transferred to Les Arcs. I didn't get back home until after dark. I slept that night for twelve hours.

So much for melatonin!

Alexis Meets His Match

The following year, the olives were also a bust, but not because of me. Extreme drought in spring inhibited pollination, and continued drought during the summer shriveled the few olives that had formed to half their normal size. It was clear there would be nothing to harvest come autumn.

"You're not going to believe what's happened to Alexis," Chantal told us one afternoon. "He's married an American!"

That was certainly a surprise, especially given Alexis's hostility toward my countrymen and his inability to speak or understand English.

"What's her name? How did that happen?" I asked.

"Lisa. It's not clear how it happened. We need to find out."

"Are they here now?"

"They're coming down next week."

"So let's do a dinner at Les Sources to welcome her."

Lisa Claiborne was a far cry from the other women Alexis had brought to the sheep farm. She was much closer to him in age—probably in her mid-fifties, to Alexis's sixty-eight—and had had a long career as a model and communications executive in Paris. She was stunningly beautiful, tall, elegant, and well spoken in both English and French. She had the high cheekbones and domed forehead that frequently graced women with a dram of American Indian blood. And she had a ready laugh.

"Alexis didn't realize when he married me that he would have to do some remodeling," she said as we sipped champagne in the mistral room.

Normally, if you suggested that Alexis spend money, he would turn sullen, if not openly hostile. Instead, he just smiled and stroked her long auburn hair. "Anything for you, dear."

"So, what are you planning to do?" Chantal asked.

"Air-conditioning," Lisa said. "I couldn't get to sleep last night."

"Mais non, *chérie*," Alexis said. "That wasn't why you couldn't get to sleep last night."

She wagged a finger at him, then wiggled her glass at me to fill it up.

"We need to install a bathtub. You can't have a house with just a shower."

"You have an entire swimming pool you can bathe in," Alexis said.

"But chéri, that won't be of any use once it gets cold."

It went on like that for the entire evening, chéri this, and chérie that, the two of them practically cooing at each other from across the table. But I sensed from her comments about the AC and the bath that Lisa was a material woman.

After everyone went home and we were cleaning up, Christina turned to me with a glint in her eye.

"He's seriously gone," she said. "Did you hear that? He's become a doormat."

"Let's see how long it lasts."

It was certainly true that we had never seen Alexis behave like this with anyone, and Lisa appeared to be the cause of his transformation.

"If I said *chéri, chéri* to you, you'd walk out on me," Christina said.

"But that's me," I said. "We're both a little rough around the edges."

When Alexis invited us for dinner the following week, we were even more astonished. Lisa wanted to show off the improvements she had made to the house. Both the bathtub and the AC were already installed.

"That was quick," I remarked once we had returned to the pergola outside where Alexis was serving champagne.

"Ah, what can I say. Life is short. And love… love!"

"Love, what, chéri?" Lisa said, inserting her

arm around his waist and nuzzling up to his cheek.

"*Ah-ah-ah!*" he groaned. "I think I am going crazy."

"Not crazy. Just happy, chéri. You have not had anyone in years to actually make you happy."

Alexis had bought ostrich steaks and cooked them to perfection on the grill, pink in the center with pink juice spilling out onto the plates.

"So now that everything goes well and everyone is so happy," Thierry said, "are you going to make up with Albert?"

Alexis lost his smile as quickly as if he had just fallen into a tub of ice water. "*Non!*" he said forcefully. "This is not a person, as far as I am concerned. You are talking about a ghost."

Lisa turned to me and actually winked.

"Chéri, how can you say that? The two of you have been such good friends for so long. You told me that yourself. Surely that is more important than just a little argument over money?"

He looked at us helplessly and eventually threw up his hands.

"Okay, okay. I'll talk to Albert. The rat."

"Chéri, no. You'll talk to Albert nicely."

"*Ah-ah-ah….* What am I going to become?" he moaned. But it was a moan of pleasure.

The Regatta

Every year in the first week of October after the gawkers and the tourists have gone home, the city of Saint-Tropez hosts a regatta that has got to be one of the most extravagant in the world. It began decades ago as a luncheon wager between two sailing buddies who raced each other from the town harbor to the Club Cinquante-Cinq, making their turn at the Nioulargue buoy ten kilometers off the coast of Pampelonne Beach. The loser was supposed to buy lunch. But they got off to such a late start, and the club was on its last service, that they radioed each other to head straight to the restaurant. Now it's called Les Voiles de Saint-Tropez. I have never seen so many boats in the water at one time in my life. There were hundreds of sails upon the low, rolling white-crested waves.

Bob and Christine, our former neighbors from Beauvallon, invited me to tour the regatta in their single-engine runabout. They met me at the boat slip in Sainte-Maxime just before 11:00 a.m. We motored out into the bay, where enormous sailboats were plying the waters in every direction, along with hundreds of smaller boats. Some of them were three-mast equivalents of the 152-foot Mangusta yachts that always lingered in the harbor. We motored in and around them, waving to the crews, taking pictures. It was more congested than the Champs-Élysées circling the Arc de Triomphe and just as chaotic. I didn't see any buoys or course markers.

"Where's the race?" I asked Bob.

"It doesn't start until after lunch," he said. "This is just *pour la frime*—showing off."

Bob was of course Robert, but he used the Americanism, as did a number of Frenchmen I had known who lived through World War II in proximity to American GIs. Born in Oran, Algeria, he was a *pied-noir*, a term that has no equivalent in English. It meant a Frenchman born in the North African colonies who returned to Mother France after independence in the 1960s.

"I learned English cadging chocolate bars from the GIs who landed in Oran," he said. "They were just kids—but I was even younger, so that never dawned on me. To me, they were like gods, with their pressed uniforms and helmets and boots. My mother adored them."

Bob was a supporter of Jean-Marie Le Pen and liked to badger me about the war in Iraq, which Le Pen had opposed.

"Just before you Americans went into Iraq, Le Pen was in Baghdad talking to Saddam to prevent the war," he said.

"Saddam must not have paid him enough," I said.

"Mais non," he groaned. "You've got it all wrong. It was never about the money."

"Really? I seem to remember that Le Pen got an oil concession from Saddam during the oil-for-food scandal."

"That's just an invention of your CIA," Bob said.

Now, when you read that exchange, you might think we were in the midst of an argument, but we were not. This was just friendly banter. Bob liked to pretend that I was an undercover CIA officer, a "fact" that explained the time I had spent in Iraq investigating French arms sales.

"We knew all about you," he said. "Our DGSE was tracking every one of you CIA guys."

"You certainly made more money off of Saddam than the Americans ever did," I said.

"That's true. Isn't that so, *kiki*?" he said, turning to his wife. "If Saddam were still there, I never would have retired. We'd be living in a palace along the Tigris."

"*You'd* be living in a palace along the Tigris," Christine corrected him. "I'd be living in Paris."

Bob had owned a small company that cashed in on the French arms bonanza to sell police and internal security gear to Saddam. It was a niche market the French arms giants disdained, crumbs beneath the table. But those crumbs were enough to finance a comfortable retirement for them.

Christine was my age, nearly twenty years younger than Bob. From time to time, she would pretend exasperation at his political teasing and xenophobic rants, but I think she secretly enjoyed it. Bob always had something to say and had worked in many of the foreign hellholes that made the evening news. No one seeing him would ever think he was seventy-five years old. Short, wiry, and well tanned, he was an avid cyclist. Like Thierry, he had desert-rigged his 4x4, a military-style Land Rover, and regularly went on autumn safaris in the Sahara. Married to a sensual woman twenty years his junior was

bound to keep him in shape—or make him a cuckold. He preferred to stay in shape.

We crisscrossed the bay for over an hour, then headed up the peninsula to the inlet where Brigitte Bardot lived and cast anchor.

"Say hello to Bébé," he said, pointing to a wild area of beach. Somewhere behind the sloppy tamarisk trees was the beach shack where she lived. She was said to keep the place a mess on purpose so the tourists and gawkers would never think to associate it with her glamour. We anchored near a cement wharf and stripped to our bathing suits to swim. The water was still warm and a clear pale green from the sand bottom. It was pure delight.

We motored back into the harbor of Saint-Tropez just before 1:00 p.m., past an enormous yacht flying the Union Jack. It was so big it couldn't moor with the billionaires' yachts in town but had docked at a specially built pier—called a *môle*—that stretched from the Tour du Portalet out to the squat lighthouse at the harbor entry. This is where the queen of England's yacht *Britannia* used to pull up. I suppose the idea was to segregate the Brits from the riffraff in town. Or vice versa.

"Let's have a glass of wine before everyone comes in for lunch," Bob said.

The boat slips were virtually empty, since all the big boats were out for the pre-regatta photo op. Bob pulled up right in front of the Sénéquier and had to climb up a ladder on the sea side of the wharf to reach street level. You never saw those ladders normally since the yachts rode so high that their gangplanks tilted down to the street. I climbed up after Christine and burst out laughing.

"Your boat didn't feel so small when we were out on the water," I said. "Here, it looks like a floating bathtub."

Bob grinned. "And because it is registered in the Var, I have the right to pull up at the moorings in Saint-Tropez. At least, temporarily."

Bob waved to the head waiter, who came over and shook his hand and ushered us to a prime table out on the sidewalk.

"This is Bob's office," Christine said.

"Office?"

"He comes here on his scooter at eight thirty every morning for coffee and gossip," she said.

"Bob, tell me it's not true. You really come to Saint-Tropez every morning with the *midinettes* and the wannabes?"

"Mais non," he laughed. "I come here every morning before any of them are out of bed. You'd be surprised the stuff you learn at that time of day."

The Sénéquier was the oldest café in town, with a bright red awning and bright red chairs and tables, too. In the wintertime they closed the folding glass doors and lit high-standing gas heaters. But today it was still warm, and without the summertime crowds banging your elbows and bellowing into your ears, it was actually pleasant.

"Well, praise the Lord for this wonderful morning," I said, raising my glass.

Bob harrumphed. "You're not going to do your cinema about the good Lord," he said.

"I think Ken is right, and we should say a prayer," Christine said.

"Not you, too!" Bob huffed. "I'm not going to pray to Allah."

"We're not praying to Allah," I said.

"Allah, God, Jesus—they're all the same."

"They're not, you know. Allah was the moon god of Mecca until Muhammad rehabilitated him."

Bob pretended to be a *kafir*, *un mécréant*, a nonbeliever. But Christine's faith was strong, even if she rarely went to church, which is why she was always grateful when I prayed before meals.

"I don't need some priest to tell me what to do," Bob said.

"That's true," I agreed.

"Bob does the good because it comes naturally," Christine said. "He thinks he is just doing what he wants, but God knows otherwise."

"God doesn't know anything," Bob said.

"You'd be surprised," I said.

Bob pretended to be the tough guy, dependent on no one, irreverent, sufficient unto himself. But every time Christine left him to spend a week at their Paris *pied-à-terre*, he was in agony and frequently came over for dinner.

What he never told the head waiter at the Sénéquier, or anyone else, for that matter, was that every morning when he took his scooter to the "office," he stopped off at a nursing home along the way to visit his ninety-eight-year-old mother. And if he went away for a week, she was his first stop when he returned. I always felt that God had designed a special part for Bob to play—the outspoken nonbeliever, secretly waiting to be touched by God, who lived a more Christian life than most self-professed Christians that I knew. For all his gruffness, I never knew him to speak a mean word to anyone.

The Olive Thief

The day after the regatta I headed off to Amman, Beirut, and Erbil in Iraqi Kurdistan for the first of several mission trips to interview Iraqi Christian refugees fleeing jihadi persecution. I was also carrying a message from a friend in the White House for General Michel Aoun, who I had known for years, about his new alliance with Hezbollah. The message was simple: if you want our help, ditch Hezbollah. Aoun refused.[13]

Staging at Les Sources made these long journeys more palatable and less tiring. I was back in the olive orchard for a few days in early March in between trips across Europe with the 9/11 lawyers. The early spring was sunny and glorious, around seventy-two degrees Fahrenheit, and I worked shirtless and in shorts with the rototiller. Even hauling eighty-pound sacks of sheep manure was a pleasure. I had planted nearly a dozen small trees the previous two winters and now had more than seventy in all. While my professional life was rewarding and fascinating, it thrust me into regular contact with pure evil, the type of evil that had a human face, with real victims whose tears fell warm onto my hands as they held them. They told me unthinkable tales about jihadi monsters, often their neighbors, who kidnapped their children, boiled them alive, and then brought them

---

[13] The Iraq trip, the first of many over the next few years, ultimately fed into a novel, titled *ISIS Begins* (Post Hill Press, 2019). I recount the meeting with Aoun in "Return of the General," *The Iran House*, forthcoming.

back to their doorsteps, served atop heaping platters of rice in the traditional Iraqi manner of serving mutton or goat. Working manure into the dirt of my olive orchard plunged me back into God's goodness and his glorious creation. Just as it was my duty to bear witness to the deeds of the Evil One, nurturing this land was part of God's plan for me. I would wake up in the mornings and take coffee out on the terrace and spread my hands and shout out:

I will sing to the Lord all my life; I will sing praise to my God as long as I live. [Ps. 104:33, NIV]

Although the trees were just emerging from their winter repose, I took the occasion to try Alexis's pollination trick and sprayed them with boron.

When I came back in late April, spiritually and physically exhausted from what I had just witnessed among the persecuted Christians of Iraq, the riot of spring revived me once again. Warm, penetrating rains turned the rocky dirt green with fresh shoots. The blackened cork oaks renewed their leaves with delicate pastels like splashes of seawater. The hillside was awash with waterfalls, surging from the rocks and carving out trenches below the paths I had cut. The Bay of Pigs was knee-deep in spring milk. Refreshment time was here.

One thing about working the olive orchard in between professional trips was the ability to see the impact of my actions over time. It was just like children: when you hadn't seen them for several months, you immediately noticed how they had grown or changed. The olive trees were now heavy with flowers, so I treated them again with boron.

That year, I began keeping a log of the trees and how they progressed and what I did. I drew maps of the terraces and used a black marker to number the trees. By early July, when a summer rain made the trees explode with fruit, I went through the terraces, examining the fruit, and did a rough estimate of how many kilos I should get per tree. When I added it up, I was stunned. Unless I was way off—and by now, I had a pretty good idea of how to calculate the harvest—I should have close to 320 kilos, a bumper crop.

My ninety-one-year-old mother came to visit us from Hilton Head that July, her third visit since we had bought the house. We took her to our Anglican church in Saint-Raphaël on Sunday, then out to the rocks beyond the marina. She clambered right down to the water's edge with us and sat there in her black one-piece bathing suit, feet in the clear water, holding a parasol, as Simon dove over her head into the deep cove beyond. Grandma on the rocks. She looked amazing.

The presidential elections were that year, and after an arduous campaign that I reported on for Newsmax, I was eager for rest and nourishment. I took the train from the Nice airport just after Thanksgiving and was astonished when we pulled into Antibes and the

station platform was covered in snow! An hour later, of course, it was all gone. Albert picked me up at Les Arcs and we had dinner together. The next morning, I went down to the orchard to plan the harvest, comparing the ripe fruit to the estimates I had made in August. I was pretty much on track until I got to the lower terrace, where I was in for a shock. I had expected around 140 kilograms from these trees, with a good half dozen of them producing the overwhelming majority of the crop, but there was not an olive in sight. The trees had been stripped bare. How?

As I looked closer, I saw that the trees bore marks of the harvest: broken fronds and stems that had been raked of fruit, but no olives or leaves on the ground. Whoever had come and stolen the olives had cleaned up after themselves.

Thierry came over as Albert and I were harvesting the upper terrace that afternoon.

"Have you seen anyone in the orchard?" I asked him.

"Ouf. We haven't really been up here," he said. "I've had a lot of work."

I explained what I thought had happened, and the more I got into the story, the angrier he became.

"So someone had to know there were olives to be harvested. And they had to know that you weren't here to do the harvesting."

"Right."

"And how could they know that if they were down in the village, as we were?"

"And me," Albert said. "I saw nothing."

"So it had to be somebody around here. Somebody nearby."

"I'll ask Marcel," I said. Marcel—Obelix—had moved up from the village to a house he was renting from a neighbor. He and Thierry had now become competitors and were no longer friends.

"And what if it *was* Obelix?"

"I think he would tell me," I said.

"Really?"

"I do. He might have honestly thought that I wasn't coming back for the harvest. It's not as if I keep a regular schedule."

"But you have been here every year for the harvest," Thierry insisted. "And Obelix knows that."

While I was harvesting the next day, Marcel drove by in his twenty-ton truck, lugging his backhoe. The turn into our access road was sharp and narrow, and it took him several turns to negotiate it, so I had plenty of time to run down to the lower terrace and hail him.

We weren't on the best of terms either by this point. Thierry had infected me with his hostility, which Marcel exacerbated at the end of August when I saw him early one morning traipsing up my paths in an orange hunting vest along with his young daughter and a dog. I spied him from the house and ran up the hill after him, making as much noise as I could. He was clearly annoyed when I came up to him by the Bay of Pigs—as was I.

"Good morning, Marcel," I said. "What are you doing here?"

"What does it look like I'm doing? I'm hunting the boar."

"I'm very happy that you are hunting the boar," I said. "But don't you think you could have given me a heads-up? I'm happy for you to hunt on my property, but I would like to know ahead of time."

"Why should I do that?" he said. "The hillside belongs to everybody."

"Actually, it doesn't," I said.

"Oh yes it does. I have a hunting license and can hunt wherever I want. You have no right to keep me off the hillside."

"Hello?"

I was surprised. So private property didn't exist in France?

"That's right. Unless you post the property as closed to hunters and declare it to the municipality, it's open to everyone. Go look it up," he said.

He was carrying a shotgun, and I had nothing but a pair of gloves. I sensed no physical threat from Marcel beyond his verbal aggressivity, but I didn't like his attitude and began to wonder about cut water pipes and other singularities on the hillside.

"I will," I said. "Good hunting."

I looked up the rules a few days later, and Marcel was right. He was not required to give me advance notice he was hunting on my property since the area was zoned as forest.

When I came down from harvesting to greet Marcel in his truck this morning, I decided to eat crow. After greeting him, I apologized.

"You were right about hunting," I said.

"I know."

"So I wanted to apologize."

"That's okay. I thought you'd figure it out," he said good-naturedly.

We went back and forth discussing the latest outrages committed by the wild pigs, digging up everything you tried to plant but never digging in areas you wanted turning over. And then I asked him if he had seen anyone in my olive orchard.

"My wife thought she saw her daughter and her husband Emile out here once just before it got dark. They were carrying baskets and a crate."

He went on to explain that the daughter lived in her grandfather's house just below me, and her husband—actually, her boyfriend—was an unemployed house painter.

"It's quite possible they came and harvested some of your olives, thinking you were going to leave them," he said. "It was several weeks ago."

It was freezing cold and rained that night and the next morning. I only had a few days to finish the harvest and collect my oil before I had to leave, and Albert had gone out of town. I had several large trees to finish, and my ladder was not tall enough to reach the topmost branches, so I got a metal rake with thick, heavy claws and pulled the branches down to my height so I could rake the olives. This worked fine once I learned just how far I could bend the branches before they would break. You'd be surprised how flexible olive branches can be. They are a bit like aircraft wings, which can flap up and down almost like a bird's without the slightest stress to the airframe.

I had witnessed this years earlier when I worked as an interpreter in Paris and was taken on a test flight of a Boeing 707 that a French company was selling to an American client. To demonstrate the soundness of the airframe, the pilot climbed to twenty thousand feet, then dove straight for the ground. If we hadn't been buckled in, we all would have hit the roof. The wings were flapping up and down as the ground flew up at us and the American client and I crossed ourselves. The two of us thought we were all going to die. The Frenchman who owned the plane just laughed.

I was thinking about that incident as I pulled a long olive branch toward me and must have gotten sidetracked, because the rake slipped free and the metal claw hit me full force in the face. I felt a sudden sharp pain just above my left eye, knocking me backward. I put a hand up to the wound, and it was sticky and warm, and then the blood just started to gush. I was afraid I would black out in the olive grove where no one would find me for days, so I scrambled up the hillside, pressing hard on the wound, trying to keep my balance. When I reached the house, I couldn't find the key. By now I was beginning to feel woozy. I searched my pockets with my free hand, but no key. I was thinking: *If I have split my forehead open, I am going to need stitches, so I need to get into the house, take a look, and then drive down to the village. In the meantime, I have to stop the bleeding.* I went to the outdoor faucet and daubed ice-cold water from the overflowing watering can on the wound. Although my hand was covered in blood, it was less than I had feared.

I found an old T-shirt in a drawer in the garage and used it to staunch the blood. I figured that the key to the house must have slipped out of my pocket as I was bending down to pick up olives that had fallen outside the net, so with a crude head bandage, I retraced my steps. Halfway down the hill, I reached into my left back pocket— which I had patted down three times—and found the key. When I finally inspected the wound in the bathroom mirror, I realized how lucky I was. If the rake had hit just a bit lower, it would have put out my eye. God's faithfulness was extraordinary, palpable, and very real, I thought. Once again, he had sent his angels to protect me. Truly, I would have been dead many times over without them.

THIERRY PICKED ME UP ON MONDAY, and we stacked my crates into the back of his Toyota Land Cruiser. Before we left for *Deliverance*, we drove by the driveway of the neighbor we both felt was the most likely suspect. I wrote down his name: Emile Alphonset.

"The name rings a bell," André said when we told him the story at the mill. I had brought in 180 kilos of olives—a great crop, but nowhere near the 320 kilos I should have had. "I think he came in early in the season, but I'll check my books when you come back for your oil."

Three days later, Thierry and I returned to the mill. André was pressing my olives, and it was a treat to watch him filter the dark green oil and weigh it and then pour it into the large wicker-covered jug I had bought to store it. Just the smell of it made me hungry.

He opened his record book to write down the numbers from my harvest. The 180 kilos of olives had produced only eighteen liters of oil, a terrible yield.

"We had so much rain during the harvest that the olives just drank water," he explained. "It's been that way all autumn."

Thierry and I exchanged a glance.

"So," I ventured. "Did you find this Emile Alphonset?"

André cast a glance around him, just to make sure we were alone, then he turned to the first page of that year's accounting book.

"Here it is," he said. "He was just the fourth person to come in when we opened in late October, after the Château de Chausse."

"Do you mind if I take a picture?"

He left the page open and backed away but didn't say a word. The entry read:

"PRESSING OF NOV. 1
M. ALPHONSET. 144,60 kg, kg brut = 138,20 kg.
PHN = 12,10 kg[14] = 13,20 litres.
RENDEMENT: = 10,46 kg/litre
REGLÉ"

"At least he paid for the pressing," I said.

Thierry said nothing until we got back to the car and closed the doors.

"Mystery solved," he said. "Now you know where your missing olives went. They were stolen by a pig with two legs."

"One hundred thirty-eight kilos. That's almost exactly what I knew I was missing. Should I go to the police?"

"*Non!* They will do nothing," Thierry said.

"So what should I do?"

"Do nothing. We will catch *ce con* in the act next year."

"And then what?"

"We will break both his legs."

That didn't sound like a great idea to me, so instead I printed signs in large block letters that I sealed in red and blue plastic sleeves and wrapped around the olive trunks where they would be visible. They read:

ATTENTION EMILE: WE CAUGHT YOU.
IF YOU STEAL OLIVES AGAIN THERE WILL
BE CONSEQUENCES. M. TIMMERMAN.

For several years after this, we had no more incidents. Then one spring I was down by our front gate cutting brush when a scrawny shirtless man came charging up the road, waving his arms and shouting. Over the noise of my brush saw and the grinder blade spinning at over 6,000 RPM, I couldn't hear what he was saying but figured if

---

[14] PHN were the solid phenol wastes produced during the pressing. These had to be declared to the French government and were collected, treated, and later spread on agricultural lands as fertilizer.

he came any closer, he could get injured, so I shut down the machine. I took off my harness, helmet, and gloves and came toward him to shake his hand.

"Timmerman," I said.

He was a bit stunned and didn't know what to say.

"That's my name," I said. "Timmerman."

"Oh…I am Monsieur Alphonset. Emile," he said, and out of instinct shook my hand. Then he started shouting again.

He was complaining that Marcel had "stolen" a full meter of his property when he redid our access road over the winter.

"Look here! He even moved the boundary markers," he said excitedly, pointing to a wooden stake with a splash of red paint that I had never seen before.

Now, even though Emile was living with the daughter of Marcel's wife from a previous marriage, the two of them were not on good terms. I had convinced the four neighbors along the road to chip in with me to pay Marcel to redo the road, and the town had allowed us to use ground asphalt from the dump as clinker, which Marcel spread from his truck. The road was no wider than it had ever been, although Marcel *had* built up the side that abutted the property where Emile lived so water would flow from there into the ditch on the uphill side. This was standard road-building practice and protected those on the downhill side.

I happened to have the wrench I used on the brush saw in my hand, so I tapped the actual boundary marker—a square slab of granite, anchored a meter down in the earth and hidden in the brush Emile refused to cut.

"That's the real marker," I said, "not those sticks."

"He moved them with his truck."

"No, he didn't," I said.

"He stole a meter of my property."

"Well, I'm happy to call the *mairie* and let them figure it out."

"My cousin is the surveyor. He came here and showed me."

I didn't believe that for an instant but decided to humor him.

"Good. I'd be happy to look at the drawings. But Marcel didn't move the markers. And the *mairie* requires both of us to cut the brush ten meters on our respective sides of the road for fire protection. When do you plan on doing yours?" I said, pointing to the bushes hanging over the road.

"You can cut your side all you want. My side is a hedge. I'm not letting anyone touch my hedge."

"I have no intention of cutting your hedge," I said. "And I certainly have no desire to look at your, uh, *beautiful* house. But I suggest that you cut the hedge as you would like it done so the *mairie* doesn't send someone here to do it for you."

"If anyone comes here to cut my hedge, I will beat their face in," he said, tapping me on the shirt.

"Would you mind to stop shouting?" I said.

"What'd you say?" he shouted. He was thin and wiry and wound up like a bantam rooster, and took a step closer.

"Stop shouting," I said.

"No, before. What did you say before?"

"I said, stop shouting. If you want to have a discussion, it's kind of hard when you are shouting."

He was trying to pick a fight and it was pretty pathetic, given his size and the fact that I was carrying a wrench.

"There is nothing to discuss," he said finally.

"Suit yourself," I said, and walked back to my machine and pulled the starter.

Luckily, I was planning to stay for another two weeks or so, as I realized I would have to keep an eye on him in the coming days. He had been piling dirt and rocks from his property to form a mound against the road and had positioned his mini backhoe with the bucket just perched over the borderline. Marcel told me that over the winter, at night, he put huge rocks along the road in an effort to reclaim it bit by bit. Until then, Marcel had just shoved them over the side so they rolled back onto his property—or rather, the property of his girlfriend's grandfather.

I guess from olive thief to ground hog wasn't much of a stretch. In a way, I pitied him that he had nothing better to do. Life was too short to waste on preening and puffery. He probably just needed to get a job.

Albert

After Thierry, Albert had become my best friend. He regularly drove me to and from the airport, and we often dined together, visited wineries, and labored together in the olive orchard. Sometimes I would come down in the summer when we had rented out our house and stay at his place in the village. He had renovated two bedrooms at the back, above the salon with the hanging canoe, and had installed reversible AC units so they were comfortable all year round.

One year he confided that he was worried because his daughter was coming down from Paris with her husband and their five-year-old son. They were planning to stay for a week, then leave their son with him alone for two weeks more.

"I've never played grandfather before," he said. "It's been over thirty years since Linn was small. What do I do?"

He was in a panic.

"Can I bring him up to your place so he can run around the hillside?"

"Of course," I said.

He was rushing to renovate two additional bedrooms over the main part of the house before they arrived, and when I visited, he was invariably covered with paint or plaster dust.

"I don't think I've ever met Linn," I said.

When Albert didn't want to talk about something, he had a way of looking off to the side, as if he were trying to read book titles on a bookcase.

"Has she come down before?" I asked again.

"Once," he said finally. "It didn't go so well."

Linn was his only child, the fruit of an early failed marriage. As he grew older, he was beginning to regret having neglected her during her childhood, allowing his estranged ex to raise her alone under her influence.

"What about Jacky, her husband?" I said.

"What about him?"

"Don't you talk to him?"

"All he does is talk about hunting in the Sologne."

"Well, that's a start," I said.

"Ya think?"

As Christina would comment when I told her about Albert's problem, it was an old story. Fathers rarely felt the men who married their daughters were worthy. We had just been lucky when our oldest daughter, Clio, had finally connected with her future husband during a visit to Les Sources. Kevin and Julian had been best friends at college, and Julian always brought him home on vacation. When I ran for the US Senate, Kevin volunteered to become my driver, and we crisscrossed Maryland together to political events. He was wicked smart, kind, and soft-spoken, but he also had backbone, which he would need with Clio, who was a fierce contrarian. Christina and I had been bringing him to family get-togethers for years, trying to get Clio to notice him, and were overjoyed when they finally got married. So I was eager to meet Jacky and Linn.

"Why don't we all have dinner together when they arrive?" I suggested. "Maybe you have underestimated him."

"Sure."

Linn and Jacky were in their mid-thirties, the age of our oldest children. He had a big sales job in the Paris area and lived for the weekend hunts in the Sologne, an area of vast marshes and forests near Orléans where corporate barons maintained huge estates along with the remnants of royalty. As we talked over dinner, I began to understand why Albert didn't find hunting to be an area of bonding with him. So I switched the conversation to wine.

"I bet some of those places must have wineries," I said.

"That's true. It is the land of the Sancerre," Jacky said. "The next time we come down, I will bring you a case. I am sure you will like it."

Albert thought Jacky was all fluff, but the more I talked with him, the more I liked him. He came up to the house by himself one afternoon, and we shared a bottle of rosé overlooking the olive orchard.

"Albert has never forgiven himself for having abandoned Linn as a child," he said. "And Linn has never forgiven him for it, either."

"I'm not surprised."

"That's why we thought we should leave Romain with him alone. He's old enough to fend for himself."

"Romain, you mean."

Jacky laughed. "Of course!"

Jacky was probably a lot more like Albert than Albert liked to admit, except that he was a better husband.

ALBERT BECAME FRIENDS WITH HIS GRANDSON over the next two weeks and visited us less often than he had originally intended. He took Romain to the beach, he took him sailing, he took him to a water park and to restaurants. By the time his parents returned, his skin was bronze and his smile came easily. They came down from Paris several more times in the ensuing months, and we always had dinner together.

THE YEAR AFTER OUR BIG CROP we had a mediocre harvest, which I harvested alone because Albert had the *crève*—the flu. He sounded horrible on the phone and warned me to stay away until he was better.

I finished earlier that year, a few days before Thanksgiving, and took extensive notes of the lessons I had learned. First, spraying the flowers with boron in May had a definitive impact on pollination and greatly increased the yield. Next, it was essential to treat the trees for the olive fly as late as possible in July to keep them from destroying the fruit. Finally, while I needed to avoid over-pruning, which decreased the yield, I still had to cut the tops off the tallest trees since it was impossible to harvest them without risk. If you couldn't harvest the tree, it served no purpose.

Albert had recovered enough to join me for dinner the night before I left. I made a stew out of *sanguins*, a red mushroom that grew on the hillside that actually turned harder as you cooked it, and uncorked the last two bottles of Vosne-Romanée I had brought down from Burgundy several years earlier.

"So what do you think?" I said as I poured him the taster's portion.

He swirled the wine around and then tossed it off in exasperation.

"I can't smell a thing."

"Raspberries and a hint of cherry," I said. "It's made by two sisters. I met their father twenty-five years ago and have been buying wine from them ever since."

We were in full monastery mode. Shadows from the candles danced across the unicorn on one wall and washed the woman falconer on the other, rippling across the high-peaked ceiling and the wrought-iron railing by the staircase. The air was almost liquid from old stone.

"I hope you're no longer contagious," I said.

"No more than usual."

"Seriously, you need to be careful," I said.

He gave a rich cough, and laughed.

"*J'ai crevé la crève*," he said. *I've killed the flu.*

"Are they giving you antibiotics for that cough, at least?"

"Ouf," he shrugged. "What is it they say? If they give you medicine, you'll be sick for two weeks. If they don't, you'll be sick for fourteen days. I'm fine."

He showed up the next morning to drive me to the airport in a small green Peugeot convertible he had bought from a female friend whose husband had just died. It was probably ten years old, and he insisted on driving with the top down on the autoroute at 160 kilometers per hour, one arm on the wheel, the other arm gesturing as we talked. He swooped around trucks, the car leaning and shuddering, and I was sure we would fly off the road. I have been in some pretty awful places with drivers of dubious competence—the worst was probably the Grand Trunk Road from Islamabad to Peshawar, Pakistan—so I have learned to quaff down my apprehensions and trust in God. But I was half convinced we would never make it.

"I bought this to take Romain to the beach," he was saying.

"I hope you drive a bit slower with your grandson."

"It hasn't been driven much in years. It's like an old woman. It needs to be put through its paces."

"Maybe you can do that on the way back," I suggested.

Albert just grinned and then doubled over in a long, hacking cough.

"You need to take care of yourself," I said. "You're no longer as young as you think."

He gave me a dirty look and leaned into the steering wheel like a fiend, so I gave up.

We didn't embrace when he dropped me off, acknowledgment that he was still sick. I was glad to feel solid ground beneath my feet.

"Please tell me you will drive slower on the way home," I said.

He just laughed, and coughed.

"You need to take care of yourself," I said again. "You should be taking antibiotics."

Those were the last words I ever spoke to him.

THREE WEEKS LATER, I got a call in the States from Chantal.

"Did you hear about Albert?" she said.

"Oh my God. No. What?"

"He left his house to walk to the store and dropped dead in the street. The baker's wife found him. They said it was a heart attack."

"I'll bet it wasn't a real heart attack," I said. "I'll bet he died of the flu—*il a crevé de la crève.*"

I told her of my warning to him when he dropped me off at the airport.

"That was Albert all over," she said. "He never believed in doctors. He never took medicine."

"Except for wine," I said.

"Except for wine. I bet you're going to miss him, Ken."

"I am," I said.

And I still do. Farewell, dear friend! The Lord knew your heart and will give you peace one way or another. I miss you, still.

Seasonal Pleasures

The truffle market was not the only seasonal event that marked the passing of the years and the perennity of the Provençal culture and economy. One of my favorites, to which Bob and Christine introduced me, was the autumn Chestnut Festival in Collobrières, a village enfolded by mountains in the hinterland of the Var, a thirty-minute drive to the sea. Centuries earlier Collobrières had been the regional capital of the Maures, as the local mountains were called, and vestiges of that former glory could be found in its stately church, private mansions (called *hôtels*), and the long promenade along the Réal Collobrier, a glorified stream that had once been a sewer, marked by low Roman bridges and the terraces of more than a dozen restaurants.

Christina had actually discovered Collobrières our first autumn here and drove up from Grimaud to visit the Cistercian monastery with Diana and Simon when I was off somewhere in the Middle East.

"I'm never going on that road again," she said when I proposed she join us for the ride.

"Bob will be driving."

"I don't care who's driving. You just come back in one piece."

It's true that the road through the mountains was narrow and full of blind curves, and if you were on the outside and suddenly encountered a car you could get pushed off the cliff and roll for hundreds of meters before crashing into the riverbed below. The good thing was that few tourists—especially, few Belgians—ever came on it,

especially in the autumn. The Belgians drove with the blind convic-
tion they would never encounter another vehicle. Or maybe they were
just blind. Even in small cars, they drove smack in the middle of the
road. I'm not kidding. If somebody was headed straight at you in the
middle of the road, nine times out of ten the car had a red Belgian
license plate. It never failed.

"There's no traffic this time of year. And we're eating boar."

"No!"

Sometimes I teased her when she dug in her feet like that, but not
about driving. She had a blue terror of feeling the car slide on gravel,
as it had when she was eighteen and nearly died in the arms of a boyfriend driver in the Swedish countryside.

People came from all across the region for the Chestnut Festival, so we left the car at the end of the village and walked in. Local
artisans had set up tables on both sides of the street selling chestnut products, hunting paraphernalia, and market fare. Some offered
sweet chestnut paste, chestnut butter, and chestnut syrup, ready to
taste on bits of bread. Others had wicker baskets piled with dried
sausages made from boar or venison. Still others sold hunting knives,
machetes, hunting caps, and vests. There were cheese sellers, trinket
sellers, and even an ironsmith with stamped wall ornaments shaped
like the boar. The streets were packed, and it was slow going.

"Where are Didier and Marie-Claude?" Bob shouted to Christine.

"I don't see them," she said.

These were the friends we were supposed to meet for lunch. They
owned a bakery in a village near Bormes-les-Mimosas, on the far side
of the mountains and accessible from a much wider road. We eventually found them along the river. They had managed to drive all the
way into town on their scooter and were just locking up and taking
off their helmets.

"You're just in time," Didier said.

At eleven thirty, the local hunt club had scheduled a recital in
front of the town hall. Didier led us through back streets until we
emptied out into a square surrounded by plane trees, framed by a

flag-draped official building at one end and a cupid-spouting fountain at the other. The musicians, all men, were dressed in ruffled white
shirts, black trousers, red sashes, and peaked caps, and their instruments ranged from long and straight to curlicued like a ram's horn,
all of them polished brass. It was as if we had emerged onto the set
of *Robin Hood* or some mossy romance in eighteenth-century Britain.

A hush fell over the square when the horn players started to belt
out their fanfares with brassy flatulence, the ancient quavering call of
the hunt. You could almost see horses jumping hedges, their mouths
dripping with foam, and riders in fancy dress flicking their whips
and dogs howling and foxes fleeing. They went on and on, serene and
stately, chorus after chorus, and the hollow, round tones echoed back
at us from distant streets.

Next, a group of mounted horsemen entered the square, and after
them, a twenty-something woman in knee-high boots and skin-tight
riding pants and a formal moss-green coat and tails. Her dark blonde
hair was swept behind her neck under a black helmet, and she strut-
ted toward the far side of the square with stoic authority, holding a
whip but not using it, leading a pack of bloodhounds. She cast one

glance back at the dogs, ordering them to sit, all twenty of them; then she retrieved a bucket from one of the riders and began walking away from them as they caught the scent and started bawling. They were desperate for release, but she held them at bay with her whip. She entered a narrow street just beyond the square, and we followed her, hugging the walls, when she dumped the contents of the bucket onto the cobblestones.

"Kiki, don't move!" Bob said, tugging his wife's arm.

"Yuck," said Marie-Claude.

For what she spread out on the cobblestones was the reward to the bloodhounds for their obedience, perhaps a dozen whole beef livers, raw and bleeding like expelled placentas. The girl broke her careful choreography with a crack of the whip, and the bloodhounds flew past us, howling and bawling, toenails clattering on the stones, struggling against each other for the liver. When they reached the food, they became like a school of piranhas, ripping it apart, snatching morsels from each other's mouths, dripping with blood, in an ancient pantomime of the kill.

Lunch began at one along the Réal, and luckily Didier had reserved a table along with yet more friends because all the restaurants were packed.

"Hey, hey, CIA," Bob said, loud enough for everyone to hear.

I played along with him. "Hey, what?"

"You can have anything you want for lunch. My treat."

I looked at the menus spread around the table. They were serving two entrées: a venison terrine and pureed trout soufflé, no need to choose, and for the main course, *une daube de sanglier*—boar stewed in red wine. Dessert was also preset, chestnut torte, and all of it for a fixed price of thirty euros. We drank pitcher after pitcher of a dark tannic red wine from the region and had to shout to our tablemates to be heard. The entire village seemed to have come to lunch all at once in ordered pandemonium. For one hundred years, it had happened exactly like this, right down to the fixed-price menu and the *daube*. It was one of the many reasons I loved this part of France.

OUR VILLAGE HAD ITS OWN AUTUMN FESTIVAL in September, to celebrate the grape harvest and the first pressing of the juice. The main
attraction was the wine master, dressed in a red leather apron, stirring a giant simmering pot of new grape juice at the top of the main
square. The idea was to rapidly induce fermentation, while making a
special cooked drink for the festival. Once it began to foam, the wine
master scooped up the hot mixture with a giant ladle and poured it
into plastic pitchers to cool. Sometimes, he just dipped the pitchers
directly into the vat when the line of people waiting to be served was
too long. Behind him, barefoot children were stomping grapes in a
wooden press up on a dais, the clear juice trickling into containers
that women in Provençal costumes poured into the vat. They wore
long, colorful dresses and white lace head coverings and aprons. Later,
after everyone had drunk their fill, they performed traditional group
dances in the middle of the square. The juice, once it was cool enough
to drink, was pale and remarkably sweet. Wine it definitely was not.
But the village elders let what remained ferment for two months into
vin cuit and drank it at Christmas.

My favorite acquaintance at these and other gatherings on the town square was the *doyenne* of the village, a ninety-nine-year-old woman named Lilly. She had a round face with rouged cheeks and always wore bright red lipstick and a sun hat. Two young escorts—in their late seventies—would accompany her as she made the rounds so people could salute her and she could nod and exchange greetings with them, queen of the realm. She carried a cane but rarely used it.

"And how are we today, Miss Lilly?" people would ask.

"I can't complain," she'd reply. "And if I could, I'd stay home."

When she would let me, I would sit with her out in the square.

"So, Miss Lilly," I asked once. "What's the secret of a long and happy life?"

She tittered. "I'm too old for *that*," she said, and tittered again.

"So, besides *that*," I said.

"It's simple. Two glasses of rosé with lunch, and pastis every afternoon at six o'clock. I have never missed a day in the past eighty years. And neither should you, young man!"

We had other festivals in the village that brought out the faithful Christians who remained. Every Sunday, on their way to Mass, they would pass the gauntlet of the *mécreants*—the unbelievers—who sat in the sun on benches along the curve in the road. After Mass, they would pass them a second time on their way to coffee or an early lunch. Rarely, if ever, did the two groups salute one other. It was a division that had sprung up with the Revolution and had only grown stronger as France became a formerly Christian nation.

One of my favorites was the Festival of Saint Peter, the patron saint of the village, whose gilt statue adorns the local church. We would start at church and walk in procession to the roofless remains of Saint Peter's chapel in the vineyards at the outskirts of town, where we would recite Bible verses and sing.

Another, in springtime, also began at the church with an entreaty to the Lord to fecundate the earth, with Provençal hymns sung by villagers in traditional dress. After the service, we moved to the little square outside, where they would burn the *sarments*. These were the previous year's growth of vine that winegrowers pruned in late February and burned to prevent disease. It reminded me of the pagan wren hunt ceremonies in Celtic folklore, where the villagers would parade a straw scapegoat to the edge of town at the end of winter and set it on fire, banishing death by burning it, as it were. The local poet, dressed like someone out of *Le Château de Ma Mère*, would recite verses in Provençal and then explain in French his efforts to keep the language alive and tell us how we could support them. And then they would douse the twig fire and head off to the main square for the town cocktail. The villagers called it the Festival of Saint-Pons, a Roman senator converted to Christianity who gave his name to the elementary school and was said to protect the countryside.

But by far the most spectacular of our local celebrations, and the one dearest to my own heart, was the August 15 parade to commemorate the liberation of Provence we had first learned about from Madame Bardot when we bought the property. Over the years, I hunted down local chronicles of the Nazi occupation of the south of

France and of the August 1944 liberation. It stretched across beach fronts many times longer than the Normandy invasion, from Toulon all the way to Cannes, more than one hundred miles. At the Col de Vignon, the notch that cut through Hard Glue Mountain to the hinterlands of Les Arcs and La Garde-Freinet, was a commemorative plaque to two American paratroopers who had been executed by the Nazis just days before the August 15 landing. Both of them had French names.

Through my reading I discovered that they were actually from Haiti and were among the first black paratroopers in the US Army. Because they were native French speakers, they had been selected to parachute behind enemy lines to liaise with the local Resistance fighters in Les Arcs. As one of the town councillors explained at a June 18 cocktail, "A collaborator turned them in and they were executed. There was no way the Nazis could have found them in the maquis otherwise."

Knowing the mountain as I did, I agreed. There were literally thousands of places where they could hide, and thousands of places where Resistance fighters could pick off any Nazi patrol that dared set foot in the maquis. But this was France, and there was always a rat. If only they had held out two more days!

The parade seemed to get bigger every time I watched it. This year, my mother, now ninety-three, had returned to visit, so we took her down to the village and found a spot across the street from the benches of the *mécreants* at the entry to town. First came the jeeps, actual World War II Willys, open-topped with US Army stars, some of them without doors. Driving them were GIs in WWII uniforms, waving

to the crowds just as they had done at the liberation. Next came canvas-backed trucks and half-tracks and armored cars and ambulances playing their sirens, then the old black Citroëns with great gap-toothed grills, running boards, and signs reading ffi taped to the doors, and red-lipsticked women dressed like mob dolls waving out the windows.

My mother didn't need the expansion (Forces Françaises de l'Intérieur) to understand that these were the French Resistance fighters, and I could see tears forming in her eyes as the memories flooded back. She had been a young army wife, stationed at Fort Bliss, Texas, when her husband went off to war. Their two-room house at the edge of camp was right on the Mexican border, so before leaving on deployment, my dad taught her to shoot.

They went out at dusk, when the Mexicans were lurking in the scrubland, getting ready to make their nightly raid on the camp. Dad lined up beer cans on the post-rail fence behind the house and coached her as she handled his M1911 service pistol. The .45 had quite a kick, and my mother was small—barely five foot two—but she learned to grip it hard with two hands and turned out to be quite a shot. *Pling, pling pling* went the beer cans as they flew off the fence post. Every evening for a week he took her out to shoot. I brought her to a campaign rally once with Second Amendment supporters and had her recite this story to them, and she ended it as she had always ended it when she told it to the family: "And those Mexicans never came back, not even once," she said. "This tiny woman could fend for herself. She could shoot!"

Groups of GIs came marching, tossing out candy, and then came the big attraction: a Sherman tank. We could hear it beyond the curve of the main street before we could see it, the giant engine revving, the metal treads clanking. It came into view belching black smoke, with American and French flags flying on the mudguards. French Resistance fighters had clambered up on top, front and back, and standing in the turret was the parish priest, potbellied and jovial, in black cassock and white collar, spearing out miniature American flags and blessing the crowd. Everyone was cheering, and my mother proudly waved the flags I picked up and gave her. She could have been a twenty-something military wife all over again, witnessing the boys come home. She was thrilled.

The parade route required the participants to negotiate a sharp right-hand turn at the bottom of the village, and the tank driver had to back and fill to make it around. But that was child's play compared to the wrecker that followed. It was twice as long as the Sherman, and just as high.

"He's never going to make it," my mother said.

"They've done this before," I said. "But it's close, for sure."

If the driver missed, the enormous crane on top of his vehicle would swing against the buildings fronting the street, taking out windows and probably stones as well. Folks were leaning out of second-story windows watching the parade and ducked inside as the crane approached. The driver backed and filled, and on the third try made it around. The entire parade then circled behind the market square and made a second run through the village before heading to the parking lot so the kids could climb over the vehicles while their parents enjoyed a glass of rosé by town hall.

I don't know how many groups of reenactors were involved in these parades, but we saw the same bunch later that afternoon in Sainte-Maxime. Nearly every village in the region had some form of parade to commemorate the liberation, as well as their own war memorials, usually by the sea.

One year I wrote an article for Newsmax about the parade and spoke to some of the reenactors. "We do this so our children and our grandchildren will never forget," one of them told me. "Never forget the occupation, never forget the sacrifices of the Americans and the other allies to liberate our country. Our freedom didn't come cheap, and we didn't purchase it by ourselves alone. Without the Americans, we would be speaking German today."

I heard the same thing from Frenchmen and women in Normandy whenever I went there for D-Day celebrations. This was *la France profonde*, the real France. And just like the American heartland, they still valued grit, hard work, and the simple pleasures that redeemed their country from its elites. But fewer and fewer of them worshipped the Lord, and it created a gaping emptiness that no amount of unbelievable wine and inventive food could fill.

Plucked Like a Pigeon

When we first bought this house, we thought Ofilio, the Corsican caretaker, was setting us up so he could pluck us like pigeons, buying into all kinds of expensive services we didn't need but that he and his friends could provide.

As it turned it, we weren't the ones who got plucked.

It was Alexis.

Lisa, his American wife, convinced him after a year or two of marriage to sell the sheep farm and retire from his dental practice. The long hours were killing him, she said. It's time you just enjoyed yourself, chéri. He agreed—but only reluctantly. He had about the same amount of property as we had—sixteen acres—but it had four distinct parts: the sheep farm with the heart-shaped swimming pool; a four-bedroom, two-story village house across the street; two terraces of olives down along the access road; and a semi-ruined farmhouse up above called Les Bertrands that Thierry had been slowly restoring for him. He put the whole thing up for sale with a local agent at an exorbitant price, where it languished for well over a year.

Lisa then came up with the obvious idea of splitting it into four separate parcels. The first to go was the village house, and Alexis wasn't happy. A local stonemason bought the place and moved in with his wife and two small children. One day not long afterward, Alexis came down from Paris and was driving with Thierry to pick up building materials when they passed the stonemason on the road in the village. He waved, and Thierry waved back, but Alexis ostentatiously turned away.

"That was Bouchet, the stonemason," Thierry said.

"I know who that was."

"He waved to you."

"I don't care. He's an ass."

And he harrumphed.

Lisa came down with him that summer and explained more about her plans when we all got together for a drink.

"Poor Alexis has worked so hard all his life," she said. "It's time he enjoyed himself. He's got plenty of money if he just gets rid of this place. It's time you went out to dinner when you want to, chéri. That you go to the theater when you want to. Every day when he gets home from his dental office, he is so tired he has to take a nap. You're going to kill yourself that way, chéri! It's time to set yourself free and let me take care of you."

She stroked his cheek as she said this. "*Oh-oh-oh,*" he moaned.

Alexis had turned seventy, well past the French retirement age, and had built up an impressive nest egg. He figured that between selling his dental practice in the *banlieu* and the property down here he would have several million euros in cash for their retirement, in addition to the seven or eight thousand euros he would get monthly from his pension.

Thierry convinced him to sell him Les Bertrands, with five acres of land. Alexis had no children and took something of a paternal interest in Thierry. Still, he wasn't giving anything away. Thierry and Chantal paid a fair market price for the property. It just wasn't that much, because there wasn't much there.

Alexis had managed to get Les Bertrands zoned as a residence, because many decades earlier it had been on the tax roles as a homestead and was still on the maps, even though it was now in ruins. The property consisted of two stone huts connected by a broad open terrace. Over the years, Alexis had hired Thierry to rebuild the structures. One of the huts was now a kitchen and dining room. It had two small windows overlooking the valley, an open fireplace in the corner and bench seats along the wall, and a large soapstone sink with a single brass tap with water that came from a spring-fed cistern up the hillside. The other hut was a bedroom with an adjoining area that could be made into a bath. Alexis and Thierry would go up there in the summers to have lunch on the terrace, hauling everything up the steep, rocky track from the sheep farm in Thierry's 4x4. It was Alexis's version of camping. He ran three hundred meters of extension cord up from the house to power Thierry's machines.

The view from the terrace over the vineyards was superb, that was certainly true. But to actually move up there?

"What are you going to do for electricity?" I asked Thierry.

"I will put in solar panels. We want to live off the grid."

"There's no toilet."

"Ouf, that's not a problem. I picked up a twenty-five-hundred-liter septic tank at a worksite."

Digging into the hillside beneath the huts to install a septic system was not a challenge for Thierry. Nor was building a bigger cistern for water, or setting up a solar power system and a backup diesel generator. That's what he did.

They put their village house on the market and moved up to Les Bertrands in February, as soon as Thierry had installed the solar system so they had power. I got a call from him a few weeks later.

"Ken?" he said a bit sheepishly. "What are your plans over the next couple of months?"

I was in the middle of an election campaign in Maryland and wouldn't be able to get away until June, after my primary. And even then, I would be blocked for several more weeks since I had a book coming out and needed to do media.[15]

---

[15] I was running in the GOP primary for lieutenant governor with Charles Lollar, a US Army intelligence officer. Charles was a major in the reserves and was a good twenty years my junior, but he had astonishing political skills and convinced me to give up other plans to join his ticket. The book, which came out on the day we lost our primary, was *Dark Forces: The Truth About What Happened in Benghazi*.

"I'm stuck over here," I said.

"Were you planning on renting out Les Sources over the winter?"

"No, why?"

"We have a slight problem. It's been raining, and the kitchen is under two feet of water."

I could just imagine. The hut was cold and dark in the best of times, and now it was underwater. The definition of misery.

"What are you going to do?"

"I have to excavate around the foundation. The house is built directly into the hillside, so all the water that comes down from up above flows directly into the house."

"Please stay at our place as long as you like."

"We can rent it."

"No, you can't," I said. "It will be good to have someone in the house."

When we finally got over that summer, Thierry and Chantal had finished the excavation work and were happily installed at Les Bertrands with solar power and their own water and septic system, and Alexis had sold the sheep farm to a Lebanese woman married to a Kuwaiti in London. They bought a small mobile home and installed it on a level site Thierry carved out of the hillside so Alexis could come visit his olives, which he had not sold. Thierry was justifiably proud when he showed me all the work he had done.

"I had to dig a trench around the back and the sides of the house, then waterproof the foundation, install drains, and fill the trench with sand and rock," he said.

"What a huge amount of work."

"Without it, we would still be living with our feet in the water."

Thierry was enterprising, that's for sure. And this was just the beginning of his plans for Les Bertrands. Later that summer, Simon, Diana, and I helped shovel sand into a cement mixer so he could pour the foundation of a secret underground room he had excavated in the hillside behind the terrace. Over the years, he would build it out to a magnificent property, turning the terrace into a sixty-square-meter enclosed sunroom with double-glass sliding doors, travertine floors, and central heating run on compressed wood pellets. He built an outdoor kitchen with a pizza oven, brought in an artisan paver who installed thousands of paving stones to make a dining and reception area in front of the house, and planted several dozen mature olive trees. I dubbed it Chateau Thierry.

That first summer, Alexis came alone to stay in the mobile home.

"I've been done!" he exclaimed. "Unbelievable! I've been plucked like a pigeon!"

Over several bottles of rosé, he explained what had happened.

Lisa had arranged a trip to New York to see family and friends, leaving Alexis, now retired, alone in Paris. He wasn't thrilled to stay by himself, but he certainly wasn't going to accompany Lisa to New York. A week after she left, he got a call from his banker.

"He asked me if I had been in Deauville. I said, 'Why would I go to Deauville?' Well, somebody's been there, using your credit cards. Two of them are maxed out. I asked him to send me a list of all the charges and to put a hold on the remaining credit cards until I understood what was going on."

"So what's in Deauville?" I asked.

"She never went to New York!" Alexis said. "She took out huge amounts of cash the day she was supposed to leave and then went off with some lover to Deauville. And I paid for it."

Alexis filed for divorce, but for as long as they were legally married, Lisa had access to his money, and it galled him. She never phoned him to explain, and she never came back. As his health declined, he invited a former girlfriend, a Chinese woman, to move into his apartment in Paris, and Thierry suspected that she had taken away his cell phone. He became so worried that he went up to Paris to visit him.

"I knocked on his door, but no one answered. I could hear Alexis come to the door, but the China woman was shushing him. I asked the concierge what was going on, and she said Alexis never left the apartment anymore."

Thierry left his number with the concierge and got a call from her a few months later. He explained to us what he had learned.

"After Lisa left, Alexis had a stroke, but he recovered. Now, he felt another one coming on and called an ambulance. The China woman didn't even take him outside. He walked down to the street by himself and waited for the ambulance to take him to the hospital. He died a few days later. He had no ID on him, and no one came to claim the body, not even the China woman. So they buried him in a pauper's grave."

It would be easy to make a judgmental comment here, but as my father tried to teach me throughout my childhood, rarely with success, if you can't say anything good about somebody don't say anything at all.

Fish Day

France is famous for its apparent chaos. Try standing in line at any ski area. If you don't push and maneuver constantly, you will never make it onto the lift. And don't even think about bringing your new skis; they'll be as scratched as Vermont rock skis by noon. The same goes for popular restaurants in the Quartier Latin or movie theaters in Paris. The French just don't like waiting in line. And so, as a rule, they pretend that lines don't exist.

But that wasn't the case in my village, as I learned one summer morning when I biked down the hill to buy bread and saw a group of people milling around the fountain by the bakery.

"Is it fish day?" I asked Philippe, the baker, as he came forward carrying a tray of *baguettes* fresh from the oven. He came from behind the counter and shook my hand.

"Ah, yes, they are coming now on Wednesdays and Saturdays," he said. "They usually get here around quarter to nine."

I looked at the clock behind him. It was 8:30 a.m., and already the crowd was growing. A dozen people were milling about in nothing that bore even a faint resemblance to a line. I decided to join them, wondering how they were going to handle this.

I knew that the fishmonger would drive up in a small French utility van, a two-seater the size of an old Renault 4L, with a box of fish in the back, a folding table, and a set of scales. He would set up somewhere by the fountain. But where? I suspected that the people waiting had bet on one side or the other, thrown their mental dice, and were watching each other surreptitiously, calculating the odds.

I recognized many faces from church and the market and the annual celebrations of the eighteenth of June, when General Charles de Gaulle delivered his radio appeal from London to resist the Nazi occupation. A pair of old women in black work smocks hovered around a Deux Chevaux they had parked behind the fountain, blocking the crossroad. One of them sat in the passenger's seat, a leg hanging out the door, smoking and chatting with her companion as she surveyed the crowd. She was clearly looking for the best spot.

Several middle-aged housewives in aprons crowded about, but also several single men. I suspected one man in his forties, whose leathery tan and open shirt made him look like a youngster, could be a buyer for a local restaurant. *That made him the enemy!* As it got closer to 9:00 a.m., more people arrived, including a young couple who looked like Dutch tourists—tall and blond and a bit awkward—and then it occurred to me that I needed to keep track of the arrivals. Otherwise, I had no hope of getting fish.

Another car with a restaurant buyer pulled up, apparently causing the woman in the Deux Chevaux to move, unblocking the road. A few more and we would have the makings of a riot, I thought. And then the fishmonger arrived.

When he opened the back door of his tiny truck, all eyes were on him. How many bins of fish had he brought? Had the catch been good? Would there be enough to go around? One woman who arrived after me said she was giving up, there couldn't possibly be enough, and left. Several others tut-tutted on how few fish he had brought but stayed all the same.

"*A qui le tour*—Who's up?" he said, after he had arranged his makeshift stand on a plastic folding table.

"That would be me," the restaurant buyer said. To my astonishment, everybody agreed. Either he really did get there before everyone else, or everyone knew him, or he had so intimidated them that they said nothing. I held my breath as he started picking out the best fish—the large *daurades*—which the fisherman heaped on the scales. He selected six—at least half of the daurades, by my count. It was exasperating. But I had stayed this long, I figured I might as well stay to the end, for the show if not for the fish.

"*A qui le tour?*" the fisherman said after the professional buyer paid him sixty euros for three kilos of fish.

One of the housewives stepped forward, and again, no one complained. She too went for the daurade, finding three hiding beneath a lesser species used for soup.

Next, a woman asked for part of the large eel, and I breathed a sigh of relief. I was still in the running! The fisherman held up the giant fish and hacked at it in the air with a dull knife, lucky not to slice his fingers or slip and injure one of his clients. She took a kilo of the heavy, oily steak for half the price of the daurade.

After a few more people stepped forward and were served, I was beginning to think that everyone must have kept track from the get-go of who arrived before them, and who later....

"*A qui le tour,*" the fishmonger cried out. A woman with a pig's face who definitely arrived after me was standing near him, but she surprised me.

"Not me. It's the gentleman," she said, turning to me.

So there was a system, I thought. And everyone respected it because they knew that even if they cheated a stranger, the other villagers would put down that mark in the secret book each one held on the others. I picked through the remaining fish in the basket—soup fish, part of the eel, a few mackerel—and found beneath them three medium-sized fish that vaguely resembled the daurade, but slimmer.

"What are these?" I asked the fishmonger.

"*Saare,* a lesser-known variant of the daurade," he said. "Some people say the *saare* is tastier than the daurade, and less dry."

In other words, it was an oily fish. But it was also half the price of the daurade, and the only alternative to eel or soup, so I bought the three of them for ten euros and considered myself lucky. I maneuvered the newspaper-wrapped fish into the bottom of my backpack, beneath the *baguette* and the *croissant aux amandes* I'd bought for Christina.

Now, the ride to the village was all downhill, so the ride home was more challenging, especially once it got hot. I put on my helmet and gloves, thinking of how I would cook the fish that night.

We were then living outside of Frederick, Maryland, in a farming area with steep hills, so my bike legs were in better shape than they might have been otherwise. I caught up with a very professionally outfitted gentleman on an expensive bike, who was laboring to keep up with a younger woman in matching tights up ahead. Was I really going to pass this guy, I wondered? On the hill? What if he sped past me using his better gears when the road flattened out for that brief stretch by the vineyard? I would feel foolish….

But I passed him anyway, thrilled at the exploit, and pedaled like mad through the flats until the road curved around the windmill and the tower and I caught a brief glimpse of our house on its secret hillside. By the time I reached the turnoff, I was still in the lead and chanced a look behind me and noted with satisfaction that the other biker was nowhere in sight! I was halfway up our access road by the time I could see him rounding a curve down below.

A petty little victory, I admit. But it was satisfying all the same.

More Trees

had been planting olive trees in the autumns whenever I could find them at the local markets, but they were growing slowly. After fourteen years, the trunks of the first ones I had planted were still barely four inches in diameter, and they produced just handfuls of olives. At that rate, I would be dead before I had a dependable harvest. "You need to buy trees—real trees," Thierry said. "Come with me and I will show you."

It turned out his brother was a landscaper who lived near the family home in Aubagne and had recently discovered one of the best-kept secrets of the business: the agricultural college in Toulon. They maintained a vast nursery so their students could practice pruning techniques on different species and get graded on the results. Once the trees reached maturity—eight to ten years old—they were sold to the public for a song.

The nursery was separate from the campus, and Thierry's brother had provided only the most general instructions, so we had to hunt around for it on the outskirts of the city, far from the university itself. It was a challenge navigating the narrow, broken-asphalt roads in Thierry's open-backed truck, but eventually we pulled in through the gate like a pair of Saint-Tropez hillbillies. The man in charge inhabited a tiny office with a computer and a phone and was all too happy to lead us outside to the lot. The trees were grouped in columns and rows, graded by size. I could see oleander and flowering shrubs in the distance, but in front of us for as far as the eye could see were olives. And they were huge! The smallest had four-inch trunks, but others were six or even eight inches across and towered over us. We settled on the four-inch trunks, which stood just over our heads. The *charpentières* or carrying branches were also thick. These were solid single-trunk varietals, and most had been pruned in the Spanish manner, stretching their branches up like the fingers of your hand.

"They're beautiful!" I whispered to Thierry.

And all of them were bearing olives, making it easier to choose the ones I wanted. I didn't want more of the *bouteillan*—the large, round fruit I derisively called plums that growers planted at the edge of their orchards to distract the olive fly. I wanted *tanche* and the *picholine*, our local varieties.

"How many can you fit on the truck?" I asked Thierry.

He did a quick calculation, made easier because the big plastic pots holding the trees were stacked as tightly as possible.

"Sixteen, at least. Perhaps twenty," he said.

I was excited. As we went through the trees, the man in charge got out his cell phone and called someone to help us. We separated out the trees we wanted, and then a guy with a forklift appeared and loaded them onto the truck. In the end, we were able to fit eighteen trees on the flatbed. Thierry roped them together and tied them down, and I paid the man with a check. The trees cost eighty-nine euros each—a steal, given that they would already be producing olives this year!

We planted them that same afternoon, and it was quite an operation.

Thierry's son, Sylvain, rode the backhoe off their twenty-ton truck and *clunk-clunk-clunked* at a crazy angle down to the olive orchard. Thierry backed the flatbed until it stood on a level area that had once been a garden and ended in a fifteen-foot drop-off to the olive orchard below. Clambering up into the truck bed, he attached a strap to the first tree, cinching the loop around the lip of the pot. He then held up the carabiner so Sylvain could slip a tooth of the backhoe through it and swing it out over the emptiness and set it down in the orchard. My job was to unhook the strap and toss it back to Thierry so he could attach it to the next tree. We did all eighteen trees like this, setting them up in a line.

Thierry walked with me through the orchard to choose where to plant. "Here," I said, turning a bit of earth with a shovel. Sylvain was there in an instant, digging a hole with the backhoe. I moved to the next, and the next, and the next. There was room for a row of six trees on the upper orchard. But then I was stumped.

"*Alors, l'américain*," Thierry said. "You haven't done your homework! We are serious people who work for their living. We don't have all day!"

The truth was, I had never thought I would be able to afford so many mature trees and wasn't sure where I wanted them. In the end, we filled the gaps in the upper orchard, then moved down below and did the same. Once Sylvain had dug the holes, he returned to where he had left the trees and started moving them one by one, positioning them in the air over the gaping earth. My job now was to hit the sides of the black plastic pots with the shovel until the pot fell clear of the root ball. Once he planted it, I had to fill in around it with rocks and dirt and then water each tree for a good five minutes.

"This certainly goes faster than when I have to dig the holes by hand," I said.

"That's because you are a *rigolo*—a joker," Thierry said. "We are serious." And he thumped himself on the chest. By midafternoon we had finished, and I was stunned. In a single day, I had transformed my half-empty terraces into something that actually resembled an olive grove. I now had a hundred trees.

We returned to the truck and took a break. I brought down a bottle of rosé and some glasses and we surveyed our work with satisfaction.

"In two or three years, all of these trees will be producing," Thierry said.

"Most of them are producing now," I said.

"Just wait until they grow out. You will have lots of oil!"

The final part of the work was the trickiest. Now we had to get Thierry's truck back up the hill, and try as he might, he couldn't get it to move. The rear wheels just spun and started to dig in.

He and Sylvain discussed what to do. Eventually they decided to deploy the backhoe with the sling to pull the truck up the hill.

"The sling is rated for twenty-five-hundred kilos," Thierry said. "The truck weighs three thousand."

"Do you think it will hold?"

"We'll find out soon enough."

Thierry climbed into the truck. I held my breath as Sylvain inched up the hill in the backhoe and the sling pulled taut and seemed to stretch, until Thierry put the truck in gear and slowly it began to

heave out of the ruts dug by the rear wheels. They crawled up the hill like that, meter by meter, with Thierry feathering the clutch and the sling going taut, seemingly about to break, and then loosening as the truck gained traction. It was only twenty meters or so to where he could turn sideways and drive normally, but it took a good ten minutes. And the sling held.

"We were lucky," he said.

"What were you going to do if it broke?" I asked.

"I don't have a clue."

And that was Thierry all over. When faced with a problem, he found a solution. And if it entailed risk, so be it. Risk was better than inaction. The French called it *Système D*, short for *débrouiller*, their version of field improvisation. No paralysis by analysis here!

The Man Who Beat Trump

At the coffee hour following the service at our Anglican church in Saint-Raphaël, you can choose between coffee or wine. I find that quite civilized—*pace*, to my Baptist friends. One Sunday in June we were talking with an Englishman over rosé who told us about a couple who owned a winery in Roquebrune-sur-Argens. "They're just like you: a Swedish woman married to an American guy. But watch out: the wine's expensive!" he said.

Just like a Brit, I thought. The only thing he could tell me about the wine was the price.

We thirstily followed his directions along the back roads beyond the village to the Domaine de Palayson. The small sign indicated a break in the high stone wall that opened onto a narrow alley lined by cypress trees. In the distance we could see the stately manor house and parked on the gravel just outside.

The place seemed deserted. It was a large, two-story Empire building, with fresh plaster from a recent renovation. Large front windows gave onto an enormous dining room, with a table set for twenty, and formal gardens visible beyond. Off to the side was a square tower with stone steps leading down to what looked like a chapel.

It was after 1:00 p.m. when a handsome woman emerged and asked in English if she could help us.

"You must be Christine," I said. She was visibly taken aback that I knew her name. "We met an English neighbor of yours who told us about you this morning at church," I explained.

"The winery is closed," she said.

"If this is not a good time, we can come back later."

A muscular, heavily tanned man in white shorts and a shock of bronze hair appeared at another door. He could have just dumped his surfboard into the back of his pickup.

"Are you the American?" I said in English.

"Yes," he said hesitantly. "Alan Rudd," he introduced himself.

"*Du är svenska då!*" his Swedish wife said to Christina. I could sense she was worried we were about to ruin a perfectly peaceful Sunday afternoon.

"It's okay, Christine," Alan said.

She shrugged and turned to go back inside. "If you want to buy wine, Alan will take you. Don't be long," she warned him.

"Don't worry," he said, smiling.

Alan went down the steps to the tower and used an enormous key to unlock the door. It opened onto the ninth-century chapel he now used as a showroom for the winery. We spent the next four hours chatting—and without drinking a single glass of wine! That was a first for me, for sure.

He started with the story of how he uncovered the ruins of an ancient Roman villa beneath two hundred tons of rubble and generations of rebuilds. It all began with a column that disappeared into the floor.

"I was trained as an architect and that's one of the first things you learn. Every column has a base. This one didn't. So I got a jackhammer and started to dig."

When he bought the ruined winery, the chapel area had been divided into three cramped rooms, each with space heaters and cheap ceramic tiles on the floor. Intrigued by the disappearing column, he brought in workers and a backhoe.

"The backhoe hit a large stone, so the workmen did what all Frenchmen do when they encounter a problem."

He gave a puckish pause, waiting to see if I got the joke.

"They went to lunch," he said. "So I started digging around the stone. I dug and dug but I never hit the bottom. I tried to knock it over with the backhoe, but it was too big."

Once the workers returned, they uncovered a block of Italian marble six feet long by three feet wide and three feet thick. It was absolutely enormous and weighed several tons.

"I knew then that we had found a Roman ruin of some kind, so I called an archaeologist friend at the University. He showed up with fourteen students and spent two weeks combing the rubble with toothbrushes."

The archaeologist concluded that the lowest level had been a Roman villa, built around 200 BC, with a floor of primitive tiles made of mud and crushed stone. The next layer, with the large blocks of marble, had been a mausoleum, built at the turn of the millennium, the time of Christ.

"They found over two hundred skeletons or parts of skeletons," he said. "Those that were intact they took back with them. The rest of the bones we buried out back."

The archaeologist opined that the mausoleum had been built at this particular spot because the Romans had begun construction on the Via Aurelia, the first Roman road in the region, and planned for it to pass right out front. "They were promoters. They wanted travelers to see the mausoleum and visit," Alan said. "It was their way of attracting business."

When they first erected the mausoleum, the road had not yet been built. "So how do you think they transported the stone from Italy?"

Again, the puckish pause.

"Rolled it on logs, like a ship?" I guessed.

"Remember, no road, and it's fourteen kilometers to the port of Fréjus."

"Carts?"

"Too heavy. Carts would break."

He took us to a display table bearing a book on Roman construction techniques. Leafing through it, he showed us a drawing of

Roman engineers building giant wooden wheels connected together by the very same stone blocks that were beneath our feet.

"They used them as axles on giant carts. Would you have thought of that?"

Certainly not. Every time I visit Roman ruins in North Africa or Europe, I am amazed at the level of sophistication and technology lost for more than a thousand years after the fall of Rome and the Muslim invasion. They came like goats and stripped Europe of its civilization in just half a century.

Next, he told us the story of how he had acquired this unusual property. He and Christine had been visiting friends in the summer of 1999, one of whom was a real estate agent. "They took us for lunch at the Club Cinquante-Cinq, and I had two bottles of rosé. Then the realtor said, 'There's this ruin I've got to take you to visit.' So they drove us here, and I bought it in ten minutes. Let that be a lesson: don't ever let a realtor buy you two bottles of wine!"

"It was in ruins?"

"Worse than ruins!" he said. "There were cats."

Now I knew Alan was truly my kind of guy. The place must have been impregnated in every corner with feline deviousness. In other words, it stank.

Alan was half Danish and half Russian but was born and brought up in Bethesda, Maryland. We started talking about Washington.

"I was in the first class when they opened Walt Whitman. Today, the building where I went to high school has been torn down and replaced by a newer one. And I'm just seventy-one!"

He was my brother's age, eight years older than me, but like my brother he looked much younger than his years. He had well-muscled biceps and a leathery tan that came from manual labor, not sitting in the sun.

He began his career as an architect at the age of twenty-one and soon was working for a big company, overseeing twenty-five offices around the US.

"This was before 9/11. I lived in Georgetown. It took me exactly seven minutes to get to National Airport. I'd leave the house at 6:30 a.m. to take the 7:00 a.m. flight out. I knew exactly where to park. And I'd take the last flight home in the evening. I did that three days a week, every week, for years. You couldn't do it today."

When he was in his twenties, he designed the first ergonomic office chair, after consulting for three years with orthopedists. "No one had ever thought of doing such a thing. One of my first clients in 1982 was a small company in Seattle, Washington, with twenty employees. They said they loved the chairs but found them too expensive. They were called Microsoft. Later, all the big guys came in and gobbled up the market. But we were the first."

As he took us through the winery, we talked about the wine business. Many of the big wineries in the area had become little more than shippers, he said. "They have created a huge market and can't supply it with their small vineyards, so they buy up cheap wine and put their own label on it." He named names—some of the biggest and most expensive wines in Provence. I had long suspected as much, but Alan confirmed it. I can't imagine saying it made him popular.

He was a self-taught vintner and won his first medal just four years after buying the property. He bought the equipment from Italy and designed the winery process lines himself. He was now doing the same for a group of friends—Swedish and Danish investors, and American CEOs—who had bought a winery in Romania. "I told them I would design it and get it up and running as a friend. I don't want any money. I told them they needed to focus on two things: getting the right design, which I would do for them, and winning their first medal. Romania made some of the best wines in the world before World War II, but since then, it's like the place is still stuck in the 1950s under communism."

The winery had the feel of a Spanish hacienda, with cool inner rooms connecting to vaulted stone walkways surrounding a courtyard. Alan opened the massive hand-carved wooden doors with keys as long as his forearm. The sudden chill in the barrel room was a shock after the hot summer air outside. "We keep it at a constant sixteen degrees Celsius," he said.

Each new oak barrel cost 850 euros and was used just once for twelve months for a single vintage. "It takes the equivalent of a thousand bottles to top up the barrels of a vintage," he said. "Then we keep them in the bottle for three years before putting them on the market. No one makes money on wine unless they become a shipper. Cash flow, yes. Profit, no. You had better love what you do and do it out of love."

It sounded like the olive oil business, I thought. But I suspected Alan was doing just fine with the sales of his wine. It was an old Provençal habit to poor-mouth one's own success that I suspected Alan enjoyed adopting. But love: he definitely had that.

At the rear of the winery, the vines in the plain and the olive trees in the distance reminded him of the catastrophic flood that had swept across the region several years earlier. In our area, hundreds of streams erupted on the rocky hillsides, exploding into the ravines, gathering in volume until they reached the valley floor, where they all dumped into the Préconil. Normally a placid trickle, mostly unseen beneath river grasses and trees, the Préconil burst its banks as it surged out to sea, carrying trees and gutting low-lying houses. In just a half hour the whole valley became a lake, and the streets of Sainte-Maxime turned into choppy rivers of mud.

"Four thousand sheep died just around here," Alan said. "They found horses a week later in Monte Carlo that had been swept away from neighboring farms. It was night and I was upstairs when I heard something. I pulled on a pair of shorts, and by the time I got downstairs—maybe a minute later?—the water was up to our doorstep. And then I heard the screams and the helicopters. They were dropping down from ropes to rescue people from the water."

The main house was four and a half meters above the gardens and the vineyards, high enough that the water lapped at the base of the doors but didn't enter. The chapel showroom, however, was submerged under nearly ten feet of muck and sludge.

"We had two million euros in damage. In the garden alone, we lost four thousand boxwood. Each one costs twenty-five euros to replace. There were dead sheep floating in the water for weeks. It ruined our rental villa, the swimming pool, and knocked down the umbrella pines. It was awful."

He dug out a photo of the floodwaters in front of the house, with a small metallic-looking bump sticking up above the water. "That's the roof of Christine's Mercedes," he said. "That's all that was above water. It was completely worthless."

For months, they were shoveling toxic sludge out of the wreckage. Seven years later, the grounds had still not come back, but he had been able to salvage the vines by spraying them against bacteria by helicopter.

"Four hundred people died. Officially, they said thirty-five. But the Gypsy camps were wiped out, and nobody said a word. Gypsies? What Gypsies? Nobody came asking about them. It was as if they had never existed. I remember a woman wandering through here looking for a baby who'd been swept away. Four hundred people, and the French only cared about their own thirty-five. Can you believe that?"

The Gypsies were the nightmare of landowners, farmers, and local officials, and everyone knew it but said nothing about it. They were notorious for buying small, empty plots on the outskirts of villages next to forests or farmland, then moving in the caravans of the entire extended clan. It was easy to believe the Gypsy encampment housed four hundred people before the flood. I had seen larger ones not far from Saint-Tropez.

Because we were both Americans and had just gone through a monumental presidential election, it was impossible not to talk about it.

"So do you think crazy Trump is going to war?"

"I don't think he's crazy. But I hope the Iranians think he is!"

"I sued his ass."

"Lots of people have."

"Yeah, but I beat him," Alan said. "He stiffed us on a contract. I sold him ergonomic aircraft seats for the Trump Shuttle. Came time to pay, and he didn't. He didn't realize that my company was registered in Virginia, so when I got a judgment against him, I sent my lawyers to the airport and seized one of his planes. They actually marched onto the aircraft and walked the passengers off. Oh, and these were the days when people still bought tickets at the airport, so we said, 'Whatever's in your cash desk, that's ours, too!' Trump was furious.

"I never met him, but I got a call from his chief financial guy almost immediately. 'We're going to pay you. We're going to pay your contract, your expenses, your legal fees, interest, everything. Just give us back the plane,' he said. 'I'll give you back the plane when I get my check and it clears,' I said. So he said, 'Okay, here's what's going to happen. Every Monday for the next sixteen weeks you'll get a check sent to you by FedEx. Okay?' I figure, okay, let's see what happens. And so every Monday for the next sixteen weeks I get a check. When it's all over, his finance guy calls me again. 'You happy now?' he says. I'm really not. Yeah, I got paid, but why couldn't he just pay me to begin with instead of making me go to court? And you know what he says? 'We were never planning to pay you. We just didn't realize your company was registered in Virginia.'

"Can you believe that? Trump does that all the time. He hires some company to do drywall in one of his buildings, they bring in four hundred workers, they do the work, then he comes around when it's over, turns up his nose, and says he doesn't like the quality, he'll pay maybe sixty cents on the dollar. And what are you going to do? If you don't get paid, you can't meet payroll on your four hundred guys and you go under on Monday morning. So you take the deal."

"Lots of people were saying that during the campaign," I said. "They said a lot of things—anything they thought would damage him. But people didn't care. They were more fed up with the politicians and the elites than they cared about how Donald Trump got rich."

"What really burned me was his finance guy saying they never intended to pay me. He just outright admitted it. So I asked him why he insisted on paying me over sixteen weeks. 'Because we didn't have the cash flow,' he said. You think Trump is worth three and a half billion, or five billion, or ten billion as he claims? Don't believe it. Most of it is just the value he puts on his name."

Christine never returned, although she did try calling him twice on his cell phone. I felt guilty that we had ruined their Sunday lunch, but Alan didn't seem to mind. We wound up buying a case of his white wine without tasting it, and it was even more expensive than we had thought it would be. But it was worth every penny, and not just for the stories Alan loved to tell. It was the best and classiest white wine in all of Provence, similar to the best white Bordeaux, rich and complex, with a mineral tang on your palate and all velour as it went down. And yet, despite all the medals he had won, the government tourist offices refused to list the domaine on their maps of local wineries. It wasn't hard to guess why. Alan was not just an upstart winegrower but undoubtedly had angered more than a few of his competitors by exposing their viticultural shortcuts and commercial trickery—and besides, he was an American! It was an affront to every conniving, insider relationship the big winegrowers thrived on. As we drove home contentedly late that afternoon, I remarked to Christina that nowhere else in the world could you have spent four hours discussing everything from Roman engineering to Provençal trickery to Donald Trump, all in the pursuit of the perfect bottle of wine. I loved this part of France.

In memoriam: Alan von Eggers Rudd, 1946–2021.[16]

---

[16] As I was doing the final draft of this manuscript, I learned that Alan had died in May 2021 in an accident involving a ladder. Christine continues on at the vineyard. And an angel passed, stirring the lavender-scented Provençal air with his wings…

Little Cookie

Christina came down from Sweden to join me at the end of February so we could go skiing with our son Julian for a few days in the Spanish Pyranées. Two weeks later, she was getting ready to head back to Sweden, and I was booked on a flight through Paris to Tbilisi, Georgia, on assignment for the 9/11 lawyers, when the world turned upside down.

We never expected to live through a live version of Daniel Defoe's *A Journal of the Plague Year*. But when we woke up on Sunday, March 15, 2020, France had gone insane. The government had ordered the closure of all restaurants, cafés, and businesses, ostensibly in an effort to slow the spread of COVID-19. And that, with just 2,500 known cases nationwide.

The next morning, with a wind whipping in off the ocean, it was too cold to work in the olive orchard, where I had started to turn the earth with the thirty-five-year-old tractor I had purchased from Thierry. The wind was also too strong to use the fireplace upstairs, where I was correcting the proofs of my latest book, so by midafternoon Christina suggested we take a tour of Sainte-Maxime to see how the new restrictions were playing out. It was a shock.

If somebody had told me a week earlier that the government could actually shut down the whole country and quarantine the population, I would have scoffed. We sat on a bench down by the port to watch. In a half hour, only a handful of people walked past, two

220

of them local police. Shops and restaurants and cafés were all shuttered, some of them with yesterday's menu posted outside. The only thing resembling a normal crowd were four police officers surveying the main street from the port. Across from them, two people waited separately outside the pharmacy. Only one customer was allowed in at a time. It was like we had been hit with a neutron bomb: the town was intact but the people had vanished. *Poof!*

That evening, French president Emmanuel Macron addressed the nation. I had never liked Macron. Besides the fact that he was a technocrat, a global elitist, and a pervert—that last I will explain in a minute—at forty-two he looked like a pint-sized teenager who had never done a lick of work in his life, which of course he hadn't. So when he scowled and repeated the theme of his speech, "*Nous sommes en guerre*—We are at war," it made me laugh. If you drawled out his last name as the Provençals did, it became *macaron*, French for macaroon, so I called him "Little Cookie." When Thierry translated it back into French, it became *Petit Bisquit.*

I say Macron was a pervert as a literal statement of fact. At the age of fifteen he fell in love with his schoolteacher, Brigitte Auzière, who was twenty-five years his senior and a married mother of three. Young Emmanuel's parents thought their affair was perverse and tried to separate them, but he vowed he was going to marry the teacher anyway and wound up doing so a few years later. In any sane country, she would have gone to jail, and he could never have pursued a political career. Not France.

Little Cookie announced much more than the closure of shops and restaurants. He said the government was basically taking over the country. Citizens were to stay at home. Schools and day-care centers would close as of the following morning, as would the nation's airports and borders. French people stuck overseas might be repatriated—but maybe not. For at least two weeks, the entire country would be locked down. He was calling for a payroll tax holiday, a business rent holiday, a business loan holiday, no gas or electric bills, with not a word of who was going to foot the bill (of course, it would be the taxpayers). But don't worry: *government will take care of you.* After listening to the speech, I posted to Facebook that Macron had just realized the wet dream of the global elites and the Communists—total central government control—and no one was up in arms. Why? Because a surprising number of people believed the economy should be controlled by the state anyhow and actually cheered him on.

On Tuesday, the interior minister codified Macron's pronouncements. As of noon that day, it became *illegal* for anyone to travel outside their house except to buy food, visit the doctor, walk their dog, or go to work—but only if their job could not be done by telecommuting. You could visit family, and divorced parents with joint custody over their children could meet to hand them off. But you needed to carry a written authorization downloaded from a government website. A hundred thousand gendarmes were put on alert to check your papers! A first offense meant a fine of 38 euros, but the minister warned that the government was planning to raise it to 150 euros in short order. The government was taking these steps "not to penalize people, but to protect them," he added.

I wondered how long the normally rebellious French would accept this. My first inclination was, not for long.

France Inter, the state-run radio, ran segments on homeschooling and how to adjust to living full-time with your children. They even ran a segment—you guessed it—on sex. "The authorities haven't yet said if the virus is sexually transmissible," the journalist said, "but I wouldn't be surprised if we had a baby boom nine months from now. This said, it will require some imagination to have sex while keeping three feet apart from each other, as the government is recommending."

That is an actual quote.

The whole country had gone insane.

What stuck in my craw the most, however, was the hypocrisy of it. Macron and his government were calling the stay-at-home orders "voluntary confinement," but of course there was nothing voluntary about it.

That evening, I sent out an email to friends. "Since high noon on Tuesday, Christina and I have been placed under house arrest along with sixty million French men and women, for a crime none of us has been told we have committed," I wrote. We had been *assignés à résidence*—confined to quarters. I compared the *laissez-passez* documents the authorities now required to the papers the Gestapo made the French carry during the Nazi occupation. The Soviet Union also had required citizens to carry a special passbook if they wanted to travel inside the Evil Empire. So did the South African apartheid government to restrict blacks. It was not something that free countries did.

On day three of the national house arrest, COVID cases doubled. The next day, they doubled again. All of this showed the effectiveness of the lockdown, of course! The police had now handed out four thousand tickets to people caught outside their homes without their *laissez-passez*, for 135 euros each. No one even reminded the government that the fine had initially been set at 38 euros.

In an ironic wrinkle, it now appeared that France had no surgical masks for its medical personnel because the government sent the entire national stockpile to China on February 19 as a gesture of solidarity. Shortly before she resigned to run for mayor of Paris, Health Minister Agnès Buzyn declared that wearing masks was "totally useless" for healthy people, and that there was "very little risk" of the virus spreading. (Later, in an interview with *Le Monde*, she claimed that the whole crisis had been foreseeable and that she had warned

Little Cookie in January that the virus was about to hit France "like a tsunami.")[17]

On day four of the house arrest, the mayor of Nice announced that he had COVID and the city of Paris closed all public parks, including the bike lanes on the *voies sur berge* along the Seine where on the weekends you could bike or stroll without cars. If you defied the ban, a drone would spot you and order you via loudspeaker to return home.

In the south of France, the mayors of several prominent seaside towns decided to close the beaches. Why? Because too many people had gone to the beach when it was sunny the previous day, so they needed to be punished.

Couples began complaining they couldn't stand each other. A popular Twitter meme was circulating: "My wife just sent me out for a walk. She said she's happy to pay the fine."

At the beginning of the second week of house arrest, France Inter invited a group of doctors to compare the French decision to quarantine the healthy population to Sweden and Holland, where schools and most businesses remained open on the theory that the best defense was to build up herd immunity. One of the doctors admitted that herd immunity was a rational public policy, "but it's not the decision we made in France. We decided for a total quarantine because our hospitals could not deal with the number of serious cases requiring reanimation or special ventilators."

So there it was. The French admitted that it was just too complicated to figure out how to focus on populations at risk, so they locked everyone in the same prison.

The media, as expected, jumped all over Donald Trump for saying that the flu had killed more people and we didn't shut down the

---

[17] Ariane Chemin, "Les regrets d'Agnès Buzyn: On aurait dû tout arrêter, c'était une mascarade," *Le Monde*, March 17, 2020, https://www.lemonde.fr/politique/article/2020/03/17/entre-campagne-municipale-et-crise-du-coronavirus-le-chemin-de-croix-d-agnes-buzyn_6033395_823448.html. (See also: https://www.francetvinfo.fr/sante/maladie/coronavirus/mise-en-examen-d-agnes-buzyn-ce-que-declarait-l-ex-ministre-de-la-sante-sur-la-gestion-de-l-epidemie-en-2020_4768021.html)

economy—that car accidents killed more people and we don't tell car makers to stop making cars. "When you shut down the economy, people also die," Trump said. In France, they portrayed him as a heartless monster. Nobody cared about the economy because *people's lives were at stake!* The propaganda worked: the French became very afraid.

That evening, Little Cookie announced that his Scientific Council was recommending France remain under lockdown for another week, making three weeks in total. They "thought" it "might" help, but couldn't say for sure. So, with the political cowardice that had marked his presidency, Little Cookie, the only one of them actually elected by the people, went along with the so-called experts. "This is not my decision," he insisted, the French version of *the buck stops here.* "I am not an immunologist. I am taking the recommendation from the best scientists we have." So much for political accountability.

On April 1, the sixteenth day of house arrest, the French radio finally invited on air a public intellectual who dared to challenge the ruling groupthink. François Sureau was a lawyer who had authored a book, due out that fall, arguing that the French government and the press had abdicated their responsibilities. It was "unthinkable" for elected politicians to turn over government to so-called health experts, he said. "It is the politician's responsibility to tell the truth to the people, not to abdicate responsibility to unelected scientists. We don't want to be governed by *"Professor Tournesol*—Professor Sunflower." Asked if he believed Little Cookie's claims that France was at war, Sureau scoffed. "Of course not. While I have a great deal of respect for the military and am honored to have served myself, we are in a pandemic, not a war. This is a health crisis, not a war." He raged at the notion that the government's job was to "protect" the population, as if they were children, illiterate, or mentally incompetent. "The French people decided they wanted to live in freedom," he said. "And so we created a parliament and a government to pass the laws that allow us to live in freedom." But now parliament was refusing to meet and to conduct its business. "Even during the Spanish flu, which killed over four hundred thousand Frenchmen and more than thirty million worldwide, Parliament met regularly and held dignified debates. Today, the government has simply suspended the basic freedoms of the people, and the parliament has hardly peeped."

Before they cut him off, he also went after the press.

"When I hear a reporter on national television tell his audience that his job is to reassure you, I am flabbergasted. No, your job is not to reassure us. It is to give us the facts."

Suddenly, the radio went dead. The interview was over.

On Ash Wednesday, the twenty-third day of house arrest, the French began to fret about *déconfinement*, the reopening that loomed somewhere in the distant future. They worried they would be hit with a second wave of the virus as soon as people left their houses; besides, many of them were comfortable with not working. I thought that partially explained the lack of popular protest over the lockdowns. Little Cookie had temporarily broken the neck of the economy, and probably permanently broken the bank, and no one seemed to care because they were being paid by their grandchildren not to work.

The Ministry of Interior now announced it was mobilizing 160,000 national police and gendarmes during Holy Week to make sure people didn't flee the cities for the Easter holidays. They proudly announced that since the beginning of the lockdown they had stopped 1.2 million people to check their papers and issued 67,000 tickets for lockdown violations. Even better: they had now developed software allowing the national police to instantly query how many quarantine tickets you had gotten. If it was more than four in thirty days, the fine went up to 3,700 euros!

In Nice, the prefect of Alpes-Maritimes said the previous weekend's excesses "disgusted" him, where "entire families were playing hide and go seek" with the authorities. "So we have started *des rafles de quartier*," sending the police to patrol street by street, even door to door. The word *rafle* was loaded with historic connotations, almost all of them from the Nazi occupation when neighborhood round-ups were often accompanied by collective-punishment executions or deportations. "*C'est un véritable combat!*" he said proudly. He didn't need the Gestapo uniform to be convincing. He even sent drones to track hikers in the mountains above the city.

In Paris, police began rounding up joggers. Anyone caught jogging after 10:00 a.m. would get ticketed, because obviously that was when COVID awoke to roam the streets. To enforce the ban, the chief of police was also using drones to augment the beat cops.

What had this once free country become?

Easter Sunday, day twenty-seven of house arrest, was a glorious spring morning, with the sea shimmering like slices of mirror. *Christ is risen, indeed!* I shouted out to the hillsides. Christina and I read John 19 together and lolled about, because we couldn't go to church.

We had decided along with our neighbors, Thierry and Chantal, to break the law by having lunch together. Initially, we planned to walk to Les Bertrands, since it was actually shorter than driving up the long, rocky access road. But we weren't quite sure if one of the neighbors would call the gendarmes, so we drove.

Thierry had taken advantage of the lockdown to build an outdoor pizza oven and a covered barbeque kitchen, all in stone. It was an impressive installation. He lit the fire at 8:00 a.m. When the bricks inside the oven turned white, he took out the wood and put in the leg of boar they had been marinating for the past two days. It came out about as tender as a seventy-five-kilo boar can get. It was delicious.

We were almost delirious at having flouted the law to break bread on this Easter day. Chantal had set a table outside in the delicious spring sun, and the empty bottles were piling up.

"How come the only glasses you serve us have holes in them?" I wondered aloud.

"Because we knew you would be coming," Thierry said.

Toward the end of the boar, Caroline came down to join us with her new boyfriend, Nicolas. She was grumpy—until she got a few glasses in her.

"I would have preferred to stay in the hammock," she said.

"You mean, your *Moh*-hamm-ack?" I said.

"Caroline, you didn't tell us you were praying in the mobile home!" Thierry said.

"I wasn't!"

"Moh-hamm-*ack*!" he called out, making it sound like Arabs calling the name Muhammad, which he knew well from his annual Toyota safaris to the Sahara.

We laughed like fools and drank more wine and didn't leave for home until the sun went over the mountain. We decided before leaving to make it a weekly COVID date.

The following Saturday, April 18, the thirty-second day of house arrest, was our wedding anniversary, and our turn to host.

It had turned cold in the interim, so we decided to eat in the Mistral Room. At 11:00 a.m., I realized I had to rush down to the Carrefour before lunch. The prefect of Morbihan (Brittany) had just announced that due to the rise in domestic violence, he was banning the sale of alcohol stronger than beer and wine. It was just the type of goody-two-shoes step that other know-nothings, perhaps even Little Cookie himself, were sure to imitate, and we were nearly out of Glenmorangie, Christina's favorite single malt. I didn't look forward to a month of "voluntary" confinement without her after-dinner whisky!

Cars were backed up as I approached the traffic circle on the main road, and sure enough, the gendarmes had set up a flying checkpoint. A young gendarme with a wisp of a mustache pulled me over and tapped his hand to indicate I needed to show my papers. *Achtung*! Just to be perverse, I had tucked the form into my wallet, which I had hidden under my seat. It took a long time for me to find it; all the while traffic backed up and people started honking and the wispy young gendarme became visibly nervous that a riot might break out. When I finally had it unfolded, I started to open the window, but the young gendarme jumped back, shaking his hand, and told me to hold it up inside. Even the cops had become COVID scare-muffins.

"Going shopping?" he said through the glass.

"Yes," I said, pointing to the Carrefour.

"*Passez*. Go ahead."

And that was it.

As I came back through the village with the whisky, I saw our neighbor Jean-Philippe walking toward the corner grocery wearing a mask, as required by law. He had been a tropical disease doc for twenty years in Africa and knew more than anyone in the village about infectious diseases. He was wearing the mask half folded above his pipe, which was lit and smoking. That was why we called him "Le Pipe." So much for the actual usefulness of masks.

Thierry and Chantal brought a bottle of champagne in a matryoshka doll cooler and chocolate mousse for dessert. I told them about my traffic stop.

"Good thing they stopped me on the way down and not the way back," I said.

"Why's that?" Thierry asked.

"Well, I *could have* explained to the gendarme that whisky was 'an item of vital necessity,'" I said. That was the purpose I had checked on the form.

"That would have been interesting."

"Yes, but it happens to be true. Without her after-dinner whisky, madame becomes *une sauterelle*—a grasshopper. *Un danger publique!*"

Chantal nearly slapped her mouth to repress an outburst of hilarity. The longer the lockdown, the more off-color our humor became.

"She sometimes can't stop for hours," I added.

"*Des heures? Mais ça alors!*" Thierry said, aghast.

Chantal gave a shiver of pleasure and grasped his hand. They looked at each other and burst out in a laugh.

The sun came out, so we drank two bottles of champagne on the terrace before moving inside for baked salmon smothered in a white wine and scallop sauce, accompanied by Christina's spinach pie. I opened several bottles of a delicious Chablis we had bought in Burgundy on our drive back from the seventy-fifth anniversary of D-Day in Normandy the year before.

"You didn't walk here, either," I said.

"You never know when someone will rat on you," Thierry said.

"It's the Paris *concièrge* mentality," I said. "May 1940. Collaborators."

The minister of interior was asked on the radio about *délation*—which is what collaborators did—a few days earlier.

"He said people shouldn't become informers," Thierry said. "But."

"There's always the but."

"But if they see someone doing something unsafe, then they should say something. Ha!"

"Let's not give the *délateurs* a chance to *délater*," I said.

After lunch we finished off a bottle of 1923 Marc de Bourgogne an Iranian friend had given me a few years earlier in Geneva.

"Remember when we first opened this bottle?" Thierry said.

"We all thought it was wine."

"But it was clearly marked."

"And none of us saw it."

We erupted in laughter, remembering the wine glass portions I had served, which eventually we either finished or poured back.

"So now it's the end end," I said.

"Another soldier in the American army down!"

As the weeks of house arrest wore on, we found ourselves listening less to the news and spending more time together, just lolling about, especially since the spring rains had arrived and apparently come to stay. It was great for the olive trees and our springs, but not for working outside.

"I can give you breakfast and lunch, or lunch and dinner," I said to Christina. "Or we can do dinner and breakfast. But I can no longer do breakfast, lunch, and dinner."

"Are you sure?"

"I am ready and willing, but maybe not as able as I used to be!"

"I'll take what I can get," she said. "Did you ever think we would end up like this when you married me?"

"No!"

She leaned forward and looked at me intently, reading my thoughts, and then giggled.

"Is that all you think about?"

"Almost," I said. "When I look at you."

"I'm so glad."

It was great being in love, even more in love now than when we married thirty-three years earlier. Love was patient, love was kind—most of the time, at least. But most important, as Saint Paul said, love held no record of wrongs. If you want to know how to succeed in your marriage, that is the key. Except for her one pre–Lorena Bobbitt moment early on, for all my faults, Christina had never kept a record of wrongs.

"Is that all *you* think about?" I asked.

"*Ah-ah.*" Her singsong yes.

I had lit a fire upstairs, and she was drinking her after-dinner whisky. I was still on red wine.

"I thought you always said you married me for my brain?"

"That, too."

She looked at me hungrily. "You're cute," she said, finally.

I wasn't sure that was what she meant, but it was fun and sexy to hear my wife of thirty-three years say such things.

"I don't think you've ever said that."

"Maybe I wasn't looking at your face before."

Caught up in our work, our children, and the hustle and bustle of nearly constant travel, we never took the time to imagine what life would be like thirty years later. Truly, God had been good to us.

ON THE FORTY-SIXTH DAY OF HOUSE ARREST, we drove to Thierry and Chantal's for our weekly COVID lunch. Chantal told us how the whole family had nearly been arrested. She was still in shock.

They had gone for a walk with Caroline, Nicolas, Sylvain, and his two small children up the hillside above Les Bertrands. The narrow path, which I knew well, joined fire roads on the plateau above the house. Beyond that was an open area on the cliff opposite, several hundred meters up, with Roman ruins and a cross erected years ago. Suddenly, a blue Dauphin helicopter from the *gendarmerie* popped through the mountain pass from Vidauban and headed straight for them. They tried hiding in the rocks, but they were all wearing bright clothing and had been walking single file along the ridgeline. The helicopter hovered right over them and then flew off, so they cut short their walk and headed back down.

Ten minutes later, on the plateau, their Belgian Malinois, named Frenia, started barking like crazy. She had a sharp, short bark and would often stand barking at a stick waiting for Thierry to pick it up and throw it. We had taken to calling her Schizo-frenia because of her crazy energy. The turnoff to their path was just ahead, so they pulled the dog and the children with them into the underbrush. A minute later, a 4x4 roared up the fire road past where they had just been standing, headed up to the ridgeline where the helicopter had seen them.

"It was a hunter Thierry knows. The government has deputized the hunters," Chantal said.

"Unbelievable. Let's drink to freedom!" I said, raising my glass.

"*A mort les Pétainistes!*" Thierry shouted, slamming his glass on the table. Death to the collaborators and to the descendants of *le maréchal* Pétain. "The gendarmes in the helicopter actually called the police, who mobilized a hunter to chase after us. For what? The nearest house was our own, more than a mile away."

"They have gone completely insane," Chantal added.

The following Tuesday was day fifty of house arrest, and Little Cookie was visiting a primary school in the Paris area for a photo op. No children were in the classroom, just reporters, and Little Cookie sat behind one of the mini-desks as he spoke to the cameras. I burst out laughing when I saw the footage. What a fitting backdrop for him to deliver his fairy tales about "defeating" the invisible "enemy" in his "war." He thought his electors, the citizens, were children, who should be talked to as children, reasoned with as children, and punished as children if they misbehaved.

That Thursday, May 7, the fifty-second day of house arrest, Prime Minister Édouard Philippe reinforced that impression when he announced the conditions for ending the lockdown. French men and women must "earn it," he said. By that, he meant they had to respect government orders on social distancing and mask wearing and limit their time outside the house. Still no cafés or restaurants, and no family gatherings or dinners with friends. "Without a vaccine or a cure, we have to learn to live with the coronavirus," he said.

What an unbelievable statement, I thought. *He could have said that eight weeks ago and saved the hotel and restaurant industries, the tourist industry, the airlines, and most of the small businesses that now lay in ruins.* They had wrecked the lives and retirements of millions of French people, and for what? To avoid overloading the hospitals? *The hospitals were empty!* That was one of the more surprising effects of the nationwide quarantine: hospitals had canceled all elective surgery and nonurgent medical procedures, and thousands of doctors and nurses had been laid off.

On Monday, May 11, the government ended the two-week national quarantine after fifty-five days. In the beginning of June, restaurants would be allowed to gradually reopen.

But the craziness had not ended.

A week or so later I went out walking with Chantal and a group of friends. We parked at the Plage du Débarquement in La Croix-Valmer, a wine and resort town on the other side of the Cap Taillat peninsula, and walked the beach to Cavalaire, about three kilometers away. It was already warm, but the beach was empty, with new signs indicating how many people were allowed on the sand at one time. Armed local police stood surveillance at the casino, but there was no vehicle traffic and no one else about. Everything was still closed.

As we started to walk back, a girl approached the beach front, wearing a mask. An older couple passed by us, also wearing masks, and someone on a bicycle, masked. Neither Chantal, or me, or her three women friends were wearing masks.

"It's the weak versus the strong, the cowed versus the free," I said.

"I wonder how we'll look back on this in five years," Chantal said.

"In six months, we'll look back and wonder why in the world we went along with it," I replied.

Of course, that turned out to be overly optimistic, but such is my nature.

At one point, the beach narrowed, so we had to walk single file or walk in the water. We came up on two women in their thirties, sunbathing topless. They were lying six feet apart, socially distanced, and chatting. As we passed by their feet, the first one sat up abruptly and called out, "Hey-oh. *La distance!*"

We had gotten beyond her by that point, so she shouted louder, and Chantal and I turned, wondering if she was speaking to us. She shouted again, a third time, and kept on shouting at us, verging on hysteria. We shrugged and kept going.

One of Chantal's walking cohort, Lilly, was from India and married to a Frenchman.

"If they were so worried about keeping distance, they could have put their towels perpendicular to the water instead of forcing people to walk in the water to get beyond them," she said.

"But that's the whole point!" I said.

"*Emmerdeuses*," Chantal said.

It was the perfect word, stronger and more vulgar than "busybody," and well deserved.

"If she really wanted to protect herself, she should have worn a top to keep from getting burned," said Martine, another of Chantal's walking group.

"She was certainly red," I said.

The next day was even hotter, and Christina and I decided to go swimming in the rocky inlets along the Cap Taillat, the peninsula beyond Escalet and the famous beaches of Ramatuelle. On a whim, we drove up the back road to the hilltop village of Gassin. It was 11:30 a.m., and the place was deserted. Even the town hall was locked down, despite the end of quarantine. What made this total absence of human inhabitants all the more macabre was the well-known history of the town, commemorated in a plaque dated AD 1354 by the main portcullis in the town walls. In times of plague, the local burghers lowered the portcullis, the plaque explained, to prevent plague-ridden peons from the valley from storming the gates. Now, the townsfolk just hid away behind closed shutters as the plague shuffled and lurked below.

We bought a bottle of chilled rosé at the wine co-op in Ramatuelle to go with the quiche we had bought at our local market and headed out onto the rocks to enjoy lunch, the sun, and the sea. The small beaches were packed. It felt almost like a return to normal. People had doffed their clothes and were sunbathing. After eating, I rolled over to nap in the sun.

I was in the midst of pleasant dreams when I heard a male voice.

"*C'est interdit, monsieur.*"

Huh? I thought, waking up. I rolled over and looked up.

"*C'est interdit, monsieur,*" a policeman repeated.

Was he objecting to my state of undress? If so, I was not the only one.

"What's forbidden?" I asked him.

His answer astonished me.

"Putting your towel down. You don't have the right to put your towel down. If you want to come to the beach you can swim or stand, but not put down a towel."

"Okay, sure," I said.

We picked up our towels and got dressed and started to walk up to the car. But then I decided to go back to the rocks to see what was happening.

Sure enough, the policeman and his female colleague were going from group to group, telling the sunbathers to pick up their towels. But no one was actually leaving. They just stood around in clusters. I started to take videos of the police as they came toward me. They had to cross a tiny bridge over a watery channel to return to the parking lot where they had left their quads, and seeing my camera, they ducked behind the rocks.

"Are you taking pictures?" the bearded officer called out.

"Of course I am," I said.

"I will need to see your camera."

You can forget that, I thought, and continued filming.

When he peered out and saw I wasn't going to stop, he called again.

"Have you stopped taking pictures?"

"Sure," I said, and started to walk toward him so that we had to pass each other on the narrow bridge. I didn't offer to show him my phone, and he didn't ask to see it. I was guessing he was too embarrassed to do so, with so many people looking on.

When we got home that evening, I read in the local paper, *Var Matin*, that the mayor of Ramatuelle was boasting that he had reopened the big tourist beach at Pampelonne that morning.

"So," I remarked to Christina. "It's okay to put down a towel on the tourist beach where you will spend money, but it's not okay to put down a towel in the wild. Go figure."

The next week, I went walking again with Chantal and a larger group of friends along the fire roads on a spine of mountain above Cavalaire. The views were magnificent: on one side, a vast sweep of sea and the islands of Port-Cros and Ile du Levant; on the other, a tremendous drop-off to the interior valley and the airport at La Môle, right next to the Chateau de St. Exupéry, which still belonged to the descendants of the author of *The Little Prince*. It was a much longer walk than our earlier one, and we stopped periodically to drink water. Claud, Martine's husband, was practicing the map-reading skills he had learned in the army, guiding us with printed maps, not his GPS phone.

As we came down from the summit to a crossroads in an elevated plateau, I noticed an unusual formation in the path. Someone had piled stones in a circle and inside the circle formed the numeral 19 with smaller stones.

I shouted to the others to come look and say a prayer.

"This is the grave site of COVID," I said. "It is now dead and buried. Let us thank God to have kept us from the deadly pestilence that stalks in the darkness and the plague that destroys at midday," I said. I had memorized the NIV translation of Psalm 91 near the start of the lockdown and rendered it freely into French.

As I said, I am an optimist. But it felt good to say it and even better to start going to restaurants the next week.

The Cast-Iron Lunch

My brother Bill arrived late on a Thursday evening in July from Paris, so we enjoyed a late dinner of what I called French fast food—*confit de canard*—washed down with several bottles of Givry, a delightful pinot noir from the southern part of Burgundy that Henry IV reportedly served at court. The next day, we worked together on the hillside, cutting and hauling brush with my tractor. He had turned seventy-five that year but was probably in better shape than I was, eight years his junior.

On Saturday, after a late breakfast, we hiked up my paths all the way to the fire road along the ridgeline, elevation 450 meters, a 250-meter vertical ascent from the house. The *cantoniers* had extended the firebreak to 30 meters below the drop-off, hanging on ropes. It was so steep I climbed the last bit on all fours, using gloves because of the thorns. Bill insisted he didn't need them, and nursed his hands afterward for hours.

The view from the top was breathtaking. We were higher than all the mountains except for San Peïre, which blocked the view of Saint-Tropez harbor. To the right, we could see Port Cogolin at the end of the bay, and beyond, the Ile du Levant. To the left, the Saint-Tropez peninsula. Beyond that, the lighthouse on the hill above Sainte-Maxime, set against the sea. Looking down we could see Alexis's heart-shaped pool, and of course, the red-tiled roofs of Angélus Springs.

We had taken our time going up, and it was now 1:00 p.m.

"We'd better call Christina to go down to the village to pick up stuff for lunch," I said, so Bill dialed the number and handed me his phone. I had to do a bit of coaxing, as she didn't really feel like going.

"Will she make it down there before the store closes?" Bill wondered.

"She's pretty quick," I said. "Let's see."

We could see the garage in the distance, and sure enough, six minutes later she was backing out the car past the two cork oaks in the driveway. We now had a 2000 Audi A3, which was only slightly higher off the ground than the VW Golf. We could follow her once she reached the long, straight stretch on the far side of the valley until she disappeared around the curve toward the village. We were probably five kilometers away.

It was a spectacular day. The ocean sparkled in the distance, and we could see sails on the water. The four-kilometer climb had taken us an hour as we stopped to enjoy the views. The walk down should take less than twenty minutes, so we were in no hurry.

We were still at the top when Bill's phone rang. He could see it was Christina and handed it to me.

"So, did you make it before he closed?"

"*Ah-ah*," she said. "That's not the problem. I think the car is broken."

"What do you mean, broken?"

"Something broke off the car when I was driving down. It sounded like metal and scraped on the road," she said.

"Why didn't you stop?"

I knew the answer to that. She hated the narrow road and the blind curves and would have been afraid to pull over.

"I left the car in the parking lot above the market. Something is hanging down between the front wheels. It looked like cast iron."

"Like what?"

"Cast iron," she said.

"Did you touch it?"

"It was too far under. But it was touching the ground."

"Can you make it back up to the house?"

"I'm afraid to drive. You need to come down."

I rang off and explained the situation to my brother. I wasn't entirely convinced.

"Ken, if Christina wants us to come down, then we have to come down. How many bikes do you have?" he asked.

"Just one. It's another two kilometers to the village, all downhill."

"I'll walk. It's less dangerous."

By the time we got to our cutoff, she rang again.

"I'm at Dix-Neuf, drinking wine. Come join me there."

That was a new restaurant on the main square of the village. So we hurried down the hillside, trying to figure out what could have broken off from the engine block the color of cast iron and be hanging between the front wheels. The generator, perhaps? Part of the engine block? The oil pan? It sounded dire. And expensive.

Bill stopped at the house for water, then headed down the driveway. I decided to take a quick dip in the pool, pump up my bike tires, and change my sweaty clothes. I caught up to him just before the entry to the village.

"You're fast!" I said.

"You're slow."

"Well, I did stop for a swim and to change my clothes."

"I figured as much."

He was dripping with sweat but otherwise unwinded. I pointed out the shortcut to the village below us and biked down to join Christina at the restaurant. She was sitting in a corner in front of a bottle of rosé.

"I almost didn't see you. How did you find this place?"

"I asked Laurent what was the best restaurant these days. I already ordered for you. They are closing the kitchen in fifteen minutes."

Laurent was the grocer. I caught just the hint of premeditation in her smile but let it go.

"That was smart. What did you order?"

"*Carpaccio de saumon* for you, *carpaccio de boeuf* for Bill, and *Coquilles Saint-Jacques* for me. And the local wine, Les Marquets."

I drank a glass of water first and then tasted the wine. It was crisp with an aroma of rose petals and perfectly chilled.

"So, cast iron?"

"That's what it looked like. I was afraid to move the car. I didn't know what was going to fall off."

When Bill arrived, we discussed further. He was convinced she must have picked up a branch that made all the noise.

"Why don't we go up and look," he said.

"Let's eat first," I said. "And have some wine. It won't look as bad after the wine."

Lunch got off to a terrific start. They served us tapenade and toasted croutons and a small plate of charcuterie that we wolfed down while we waited for the main course. Then it occurred to me that Christina didn't have a shopping bag.

"What did you do with the stuff you bought?" I asked.

"Laurent agreed to keep it cold until after lunch."

"That was after you called us the second time, or before?" I wondered.

She just gave us a big smile and wiggled her glass.

"More wine, husband."

We had already finished the first bottle of Les Marquets, so Bill ordered another and we returned to the matter at hand.

"It had to be a branch," he said.

"Had to be," I agreed.

"It didn't look like a branch when I looked under the front end," Christina said.

"Did you actually put your head under the car?"

"I saw something solid with a hole in it. It was the color of cast iron."

The salmon and beef carpaccio were fresh and perfectly spiced, as were Christina's scallops. By the time we had finished lunch, we were in pretty good spirits. Of course, there was always the possibility that now we would have to scare up a mechanic, or get the car towed—on a Saturday afternoon—or abandon it completely and buy a new one, which Christina had been wanting anyway since it was already twenty years old.

We picked up her packages from the grocer and were modestly apprehensive when we got up to the parking lot. Bill and I kneeled down to look under the front end.

"There it is. That's what's dragging," I said.

"Yep. But cast iron?"

"Maybe the color."

"What do you mean?" Christina said.

"It's plastic. It's just the oil pan guard."

I wiggled it just to make sure and was able to tuck it back beneath the front bumper. It had probably gotten torn on the rocks during our last trip up to see Thierry and Chantal.

"It's just the plastic oil pan guard," I told Christina again.

"Really?" she said with a sly smile. "It looked like cast iron."

"It's just plastic."

"We had a *good* lunch."

"Yes, we had a good lunch," I said.

"Ken, that's what she wanted all along," Bill added slyly.

"Is it true?" I asked her.

She was trying not to laugh.

"Didn't we eat well?"

"We did."

"I wasn't in the mood to make lunch at the house, but you called me in such a panic saying I had to get down to the village to go shopping that I rushed out."

"We timed you. It took you six minutes."

"I rushed out."

"Not exactly rushed."

"I had to get dressed, go to the bathroom, and comb my hair. I rushed out."

"Ken, she *rushed out*," Bill said.

"Okay, so you rushed out. And the car was in such dire shape you managed to get all the way to the village."

"There was no place to pull over."

"And then go shopping without calling a mechanic. And then get a recommendation for the best restaurant in the village."

She stuck her tongue out at me and wiggled it.

"Ken, you can't win," Bill said.

I put the bike in the back and drove us up the hill without incident. We scraped on the rocks on the access road, as sometimes happened. Bill and I jacked up the car and put wooden wedges beneath it while I repaired the oil pan guard, sawing off the ripped part and drilling a hole so I could zip-tie the rest of it together.

"Did you see what skill she has," Bill said.

"That was skill."

"That wasn't just skill. That was *phenomenal* skill. And all because she didn't want to make lunch."

"Who would have thought cast iron could be so good?"

L'Envoi

Americans have been attracted to the south of France since the time of Thomas Jefferson, who made a trip through the region while serving as the US ambassador to France in 1787. As he descended the Rhône Valley past Orange, he noted the difference in the landscape thus: "Here begins the country of olives...."

He kept a notebook of his journeys and included many passages in letters he sent regularly to the Marquis de Lafayette and other friends. As it turned out, he traveled not twenty miles from our house, along the post road that later became the A8 autoroute, through the up-country valleys and vineyards from Cuers, Pignan, Le Luc, Vidauban, and Le Muy, and then down to the coast at Napoule and on to Antibes and Nice. In one passage, at the end of March, he noted that the locals "are now pruning the olive. A very good tree produces 60 lb. of olives, which yield 15 lb. of oil: the best quality selling at 12.s the lb. retail and 10.s wholesale."[18]

As you will know if you have stayed with me this far, yields like that are to die for.

---

[18] Thomas Jefferson, "Notes of a Tour into the Southern Parts of France, &c., 3 March–10 June 1787," *Founders Online*, National Archives, https://founders.archives.gov/documents/Jefferson/01-11-02-0389. (An abbreviated version, showing his itinerary, can be found here: https://www.monticello.org/site/research-and-collections/journey-through-france-and-italy-1787.)

British writers and art-
ists also came to the south of
France. Rudyard Kipling wrote
a remarkable story about the
Camargue, the marshland south
of Arles in the Rhône River
delta famous for Gypsies and
wild horses. It began as a tall tale
told among travelers at a roadside inn about a bull and was as
good a story about bullfighting
as anything written by Hem-
ingway. I found it in a collection
entitled *Humorous Tales*, left-
behind by Stenberg in the bookcase downstairs.[19] Winston Churchill also came here regularly for the summers, mooching off wealthy
friends and pretending to paint.

If you walk the *chemin des douaniers* around the Cap d'Antibes,
you will pass a villa that once belonged to our friends Alice and Roger
Eddé, La Tour de la Garoupe, and an imposing mansion on the far
side owned by a Russian billionaire, complete with thuggish-look-
ing security guards who would love to toss you over the cliffs. The
billionaire, Roman Abramovich, once attempted to seal off the cliff
walk and block all public passage, but the local courts prevented him.
Beyond his domain you will find the famed Hotel Eden Roc, where F.
Scott Fitzgerald got his first taste of the magic of the French Riviera
as the guest of wealthy friends Gerald and Sara Murphy. A bit farther
is the Villa St. Louis, now the Hotel Belles Rives, which Fitzgerald
rented in 1926 and famously entertained his camp followers, "invent-
ing" the Riviera as a playground for the rich.

---

[19] The story about the Camargue is called "The Bull That Thought," and can be read
online here: http://www.telelib.com/authors/K/KiplingRudyard/prose/DebtsandCredits/
bullthought.html.

My favorite expat was Lawrence Durrell, author of *The Alexandria Quartet*. Christina and I visited with him at his home in Sommières (Gard) in the late 1980s, years after he had graced me with a jacket blurb for my first novel, *The Wren Hunt*. Unlike the brash Fitzgerald, he lived a quiet life, writing and appreciating the region, as I did.

A whole new crop of Americans and Brits has flocked to the Côte d'Azur since then, most of whom I have no interest in meeting. They include actor Johnny Depp, who bought an entire hamlet in the village of Le Plan-de-la-Tour and tried to make wine but ended up making lugubrious drunken videos in the wine cellar by candlelight during COVID that he posted to social media.

This has been our home for the past eighteen years, and I have been happy to share it with you in these pages. I have been privileged to break bread and to share joys and sorrows with my neighbors, and to learn the rigors of the growing cycle and to contemplate God's bounty and grace.

Our new home in America is in Florida, which we have adopted with delight, wondering why we didn't move there years earlier. The homestead of Marjorie Kinnan Rawlings, who often struggled with dire poverty during the Great Depression, is about ninety minutes away. She raised citrus as a cash crop. I raise olives for pleasure. But our feelings about the land we worked and knew so well were very similar.

Here is how she described it at the end of her delightful memoir, *Cross Creek*:

What is "property" and who are the legitimate owners? I looked out from my veranda, across the acres of grove from which I had only recently been able to remove the mortgage. The land was

legally mine, and short of long tax delinquency, nothing and nobody could take it from me. Yet if I did not take care of the land lovingly, did not nourish and cultivate it, it would revert to jungle. Was it mine to abuse or to neglect? I did not think so.[20]

As I was finishing this account, the hand of Providence steered a massive forest fire that was headed our way in another direction, once again sparing our hillside. Behind it came a heat wave that dried up the earth. How will the trees fare after the scorching summer drought? I can't wait to find out. A new olive harvest beckons.

Les Sources d'Angélus—September 8, 2010

Florida—September 10, 2021

---

[20] Marjorie Kinnan Rawlings, *Cross Creek* (New York: C. Scribner's Sons, 1942).

About the Author

Kenneth R. Timmerman is the author of twelve works of nonfiction, including two *New York Times* bestsellers, and four published novels. He was nominated for the Nobel Peace Prize in 2006 by the former deputy premier of Sweden for his work to expose Iran's nuclear weapons program. A detailed bio is available here:

www.kentimmerman.com/about.htm